ABOUT THE ROYAL SHAKESPEARE COMPANY

The Royal Shakespeare Company at Stratford-upon-Avon was formed in 1960 and gained its Royal Charter in 1961. This year we celebrate 50 years as a home for Shakespeare's work, the wider classical repertoire and new plays.

The founding Artistic Director Peter Hall created an ensemble theatre company of young actors and writers. The Company was led by Hall, Peter Brook and Michel Saint-Denis. The founding principles were threefold: the Company would embrace the freedom and power of Shakespeare's work, train and develop young actors and directors, and crucially, experiment in new ways of making theatre. There was a new spirit amongst this post-war generation and they intended to open up Shakespeare's plays as never before.

The Company has had a distinct personality from the beginning. The search for new forms of writing and directing was led by Peter Brook. He pushed writers to experiment. "Just as Picasso set out to capture a larger slice of the truth by painting a face with several eyes and noses, Shakespeare, knowing that man is living his everyday life and at the same time is living intensely in the invisible world of his thoughts and feelings, developed a method through which we can see at one and the same time the look on a man's face and the vibrations of his brain."

The breadth of Peter Hall's vision cannot be underplayed. In 1955 he had premiered Samuel Beckett's *Waiting for Godot* in a small theatre in London and it was like opening a window during a storm, the tumult of new ideas happening across Europe in art, theatre and literature came flooding into British theatre. But this new thinking needed nurturing, and in the quietude of this small market town, it became possible to make exciting breakthroughs in the work. The inspiring team at the heart of the Company gave this work direction and momentum and the RSC became known for exhilarating performances of Shakespeare alongside new masterpiece plays such as *The Homecoming* and *Old Times* by Harold Pinter. This combination thrilled modern audiences.

Peter Hall's rigour on classical text is legendary, but he applied everything he learnt working on Beckett, and later on Harold Pinter, to his work on Shakespeare, and vice versa. This close and demanding relationship between writers from different eras became the fuel which powered the creativity of the RSC.

A rich and varied range of writers flowed into the company and continue to do so. These include: Edward Albee, Howard Barker, Edward Bond, Howard Brenton, Marina Carr, Caryl Churchill, Martin Crimp, David Edgar, Peter Flannery, David Greig, Tony Harrison, Dennis Kelly, Martin McDonagh, Rona Munro, Anthony Neilson, Harold Pinter, Stephen Poliakoff, Adriano Shaplin, Wole Soyinka, Tom Stoppard, debbie tucker green, Timberlake Wertenbaker and Roy Williams.

The history of the Royal Shakespeare Company has also been a history of theatre spaces and the impact they have on the theatre which can be made within them. The Other Place was established in 1975. The 400-seat Swan Theatre was added in 1986. The RSC's spaces have seen some of the most epic, challenging and era-defining theatre – Peter Brook's Beckettian *King Lear* with Paul Scofield in the title role, the Theatre of Cruelty season which premiered Peter Weiss' *Marat/Sade*, Trevor Nunn's studio *Macbeth* in The Other Place, Michael Boyd's restoration of ensemble with *The Histories Cycle* in The Courtyard Theatre, David Greig's and Roy Williams' searing war plays *The American Pilot* and *Days of Significance*, and most recently Dennis Kelly and Tim Minchin's game-changing musical adaptation of Roald Dahl's *Matilda*.

The Company today is led by Michael Boyd, who is taking its founding ideals forward. His belief in ensemble theatre-making, internationalism, new work and active approaches to Shakespeare in the classroom has inspired the Company to landmark projects such as *The Complete Works Festival*, *Stand up for Shakespeare* and *The Histories Cycle*. He has overseen the four year transformation of our theatres, he has restored the full range of repertoire and in this birthday year we are proud to invite the world's theatre artists onto our brand new stages.

NEW WORK AT THE RSC

The potential for new work at the RSC is something which we take very seriously. We have between thirty and forty writers working on new plays for us at any one time and have recently re-launched the RSC Studio to provide the resources for writers, directors and actors to explore and develop new ideas for our stages.

We invite writers to spend time with us in our rehearsal rooms, with our actors and practitioners. Alongside developing their own plays, we invite them to contribute dramaturgically to both our main stage Shakespeare productions and our Young People's Shakespeare.

We believe that our writers help to establish a creative culture within the Company which both inspires new work and creates an ever more urgent sense of enquiry into the classics. The benefits work both ways. With our writers, our actors naturally learn the language of dramaturgical intervention and sharpen their interpretation of roles. Our writers benefit from re-discovering the stagecraft and theatre skills that have been lost over time. They regain the knack of writing roles for leading actors. They become hungry to use classical structures to power up their plays.

Our current International Writer-in-Residence, Tarell Alvin McCraney has been embedded with the company for two years. His post was funded by the CAPITAL Centre at the University of Warwick where he taught as part of his residency.

The RSC's New Work Season at Hampstead Theatre is generously supported by THE BLAVATNIK FAMILY FOUNDATION.

The RSC Literary Department is generously supported by THE DRUE HEINZ TRUST.

The RSC Ensemble is generously supported by THE GATSBY CHARITABLE FOUNDATION and THE KOVNER FOUNDATION.

The RSC is grateful for the significant support of its principal funder, Arts Council England, without which our work would not be possible. Around 50 per cent of the RSC's income is self-generated from Box Office sales, sponsorship, donations, enterprise and partnerships with other organisations.

Supported by
ARTS COUNCIL ENGLAND

This production of *Little Eagles* was first performed by the Royal Shakespeare Company at Hampstead Theatre, London, on 16th April 2011. The cast was as follows:

TITOV	**Charles Aitken**
GUARD 2/FARMER/ PRISONER/GUINEA PIG	**Joseph Arkley**
KHRUSHCHEV	**Brian Doherty**
KOROLYOV	**Darrell D'Silva**
DOCTOR	**Noma Dumezweni**
YURI GAGARIN	**Dyfan Dwyfor**
GUARD 1/BREZHNEV	**Phillip Edgerley**
OLD MAN/GELADZE	**Greg Hicks**
IVANOVSKY	**James Howard**
KOMAROV	**Ansu Kabia**
RITA/NATASHA	**Debbie Korley**
GLUSHKO/STEVE	**John Mackay**
STALIN/YAKOV	**Sandy Neilson**
MISHIN	**Peter Peverley**
LEONOV	**Oliver Ryan**
ANNA/XENIA	**Hannah Young**
VALYA	**Samantha Young**

All other parts played by members of the company.

Little Eagles has been developed in association with DAVIDSON COLLEGE, USA.

Rehearsal and development supported by CHARLES DIAMOND.

Directed by	**Roxana Silbert**
Designed by	**Ti Green**
Lighting by	**Chahine Yavroyan**
Music and Sound by	**Ben & Max Ringham**
Movement by	**Ayse Tashkiran**
Fights by	**Terry King**
Aerial Consultant	**Vicki Amedume for Upswing**
Company Text and Voice work by	**Stephen Kemble**
Additional Company Movement by	**Struan Leslie**
Assistant Director	**Helen Leblique**
Company Dramaturg	**Jeanie O'Hare**
Casting by	**Hannah Miller** CDG
Production Manager	**Rebecca Watts**
Costume Supervisor	**Jill Pennington**
Company Manager	**Michael Dembowicz**
Stage Manager	**Robbie Cullen**
Deputy Stage Manager	**Alison Tanqueray**
Assistant Stage Manager	**Amy Griffin**

This text may differ slightly from the play as performed.

Thanks to Michael Colgan, Jon Foster, James Gale, Charles Goforth, Lloyd Hutchinson, Russell G Jones, Deirdre O'Connell, Jan Pearson, Alexa Scott-Flaherty, David Sibley and Lauren Singerman for their invaluable contribution.

Production Acknowledgments

Set construction by Q Division Ltd, Leeds. Props and furniture by RSC Properties Workshop, Stratford-upon-Avon. Costumes on hire from Angels of London. Additional costumes by RSC costume workshops, Stratford-upon-Avon and Robert Allsopp. With thanks to Julie Curtis and Roger Granville at Oxford University and Alan Smith at UCL. Production photographer Hugo Glendinning. Audio description by Mary Plackett and Julia Grundy. Captioned by Ridanne Sheridan.

THE COMPANY

Charles Aitken

TITOV

Ensemble productions:
Titov in *Little Eagles*, Oliver in *As You Like It*, Conductor/3rd Ilya in *The Drunks*, Edgar in *King Lear*, Ventidius in *Antony and Cleopatra*.
trained: RADA.
theatre includes:
Othello (Ian Charleson award nomination. Frantic Assembly); *The Taming of the Shrew* (Wilton's Music Hall); *Midnight Cowboy* (Assembly Rooms, Edinburgh); *Paradise Lost* (Headlong); *Hair* (Gate); *London Assurance* (Royal Exchange).
television: *Bonkers*.
film: *Love Nest* (short).

Vicki Amedume

AERIAL CONSULTANT

Vicki Amedume is Artistic Director of Upswing.
RSC debut season: *Little Eagles*.
trained: Victoria trained as an aerialist at The French National Circus School Chalon en Champagne and at Circus Space London.
theatre includes: Vicki performs and creates

traditional and contemporary circus work as well as outdoor performance and touring theatre. After working with contemporary circus companies in the UK and Europe and traditional circus companies in the US, she founded Upswing in 2004. Upswing produces modern cross art form work that uses circus skills as a vehicle for physical expression. The company produces a mix of indoor touring productions, educational projects and bespoke, site specific performance. Following events with the National Theatre's Watch this Space (*Loved Up*), The Liverpool Culture Company for European City of Culture, BBC London and the Commonwealth Games Cultural Festival in Melbourne, *Everyone's London* on top of the Trafalgar Square's Nelson column, and collaborations on National Theatre of Scotland's *Peter Pan*, and the New Vic Theatre's *Wicked Lady*, Upswing has established itself at the forefront of aerial interdisciplinary circus in the UK, and is currently touring *Fallen*. www.upswing.org.uk

Joseph Arkley

GUARD 2/FARMER/ PRISONER/ GUINEA PIG

Ensemble productions:
Guard 2/Farmer/Prisoner/ Guinea Pig in *Little Eagles*, Archidamus/Officer in *The Winter's Tale*, Remus/Octavius Caesar/Artemidorus in *Julius Caesar*, Yurko in *The Grain Store*, Tybalt in *Romeo and Juliet*, Kay/King Pelleas in *Morte d'Arthur*.
trained: Royal Scottish Academy of Music and Drama.
theatre includes: *Cotton Wool* (Theatre503); *The Glass Menagerie* (Royal Lyceum); *Stoopud Fucken Animals* (Traverse); *Mud* (Gate); *I Caught Crabs in Walberswick* (High Tide).
theatre whilst training includes: *Caucasian Chalk Circle*; *All's Well that Ends Well* (RSC Complete Works Festival).
film: *Pelican Blood*.
radio includes: *Dombey and Son*, *Fortunes of War*, *All Quiet on the Western Front*, *Resurrection*.

Brian Doherty

Darrell D'Silva

The First New Heart, Krakatoa – The Last Days, Eleventh Hour, Spooks, Lawless, Messiah 3, Prime Suspect, Out of the Blue, Cambridge Spies.
film: Dirty Pretty Things.

KHRUSHCHEV

RSC: God in Ruins (RSC/ Soho), Macbeth, Macbett, Great Expectations.
Ensemble productions: Khrushchev in Little Eagles, Autolycus in The Winter's Tale, Decius Brutus/Poet in Julius Caesar, Mayor in The Drunks, King of France in King Lear, Enobarbus in Antony and Cleopatra.
theatre includes: Three Sisters, Down the Line, Translations, Tarry Flynn, The Murphy Initiative (Abbey); Aristocrats (National Theatre); Stones in his Pockets (Duke of York's); All in the Head, The Crucible, Happy Birthday Dear Alice, The Glass Menagerie, Observe the Sons of Ulster Marching Towards the Somme (Red Kettle); Pentecost, Boomtown, School for Scandal (Rough Magic); Car Show (Love Me) (Corn Exchange); Romantic Friction (Read Co.); Emma (Storytellers); Zoe's Play (The Ark); Amphibians (Tin Drum); Studs (Passion Machine); Conquest of the South Pole (Theatre Demo).
film and television includes: Billy the Kid, Pure Mule, Casualty, Doctors, Fair City, The Clinic, Glenroe, Perrier's Bounty, Garage.

KOROLYOV

RSC: Hecuba, A Midsummer Night's Dream, A Month in the Country, Troilus and Cressida, Camino Real, Spanish Tragedy, Henry VIII, Doctor Faustus.
Ensemble productions: Korolyov in Little Eagles, Polixenes in The Winter's Tale, Mark Antony in Julius Caesar, Kotomtsev in The Drunks, Earl of Kent in King Lear, Antony in Antony and Cleopatra.
trained: Drama Centre, London.
theatre includes: The White Devil (Menier Chocolate Factory); Fall (Traverse); The Rose Tattoo, Royal Hunt of the Sun, Tales from Vienna Woods, Closer, Further than the Furthest Thing (National Theatre); Clouds (No.1 tour); Paradise Lost (Northampton); Absolutely! (Perhaps) (Wyndham's); The Lying Kind (Royal Court); Antarctica (Savoy); Six Characters Looking for an Author (Young Vic); Tear from a Glass Eye (Gate); Chasing the Moment (One Tree); Romeo and Juliet, The Three Musketeers (Sheffield Crucible).
television includes: Trial and Retribution, Bonekickers, Criminal Justice, Poppy Shakespeare, Saddam's Tribe,

Noma Dumezweni

DOCTOR

RSC: Breakfast with Mugabe, Antony and Cleopatra, Much Ado about Nothing, Macbeth, Trade.
Ensemble productions: Doctor in Little Eagles, Paulina in The Winter's Tale, Calphurnia in Julius Caesar, Olyana in The Grain Store, Nurse in Romeo and Juliet, Morgan Le Fay in Morte d'Arthur.
theatre includes: Six Characters in Search of an Author (Chichester/West End); The Master and Margarita, A Midsummer Night's Dream, The Coffee House, Nathan the Wise (Chichester); The Hour We Knew Nothing of Each Other, President of an Empty Room (National Theatre); A Raisin in the Sun (winner of the Olivier Award for Best Supporting Actor. Young Vic at the Lyric Hammersmith/tour); Skellig, The Blacks (Young Vic); Ali Baba and the Forty Thieves, A Midsummer Night's

Dream (London Bubble); *The Bogus Woman* (MEN Award and Fringe First Award. Red Room/Bush/Traverse).

television and film includes: *Doctor Who, Fallout, The Colour of Magic, Summerhill, EastEnders, Mysterious Creatures, The Last Enemy, New Tricks, Shameless, Holby City, Fallen Angel, After Thomas.*

radio includes: *No.1 Ladies Detective Agency, Pilgrim, A Time for Justice, The Farming of Bones.*

Dyfan Dwyfor

YURI GAGARIN

Ensemble productions:
Yuri Gagarin in *Little Eagles*, William in *As You Like It*, Dromio of Ephesus in *The Comedy of Errors*, 1st Ilya/Scene Announcer in *The Drunks*, Laertes/Marcellus/Rosencrantz in *Hamlet*, Peter in *Romeo and Juliet*, Lamorak/Percival/Lavaine in *Morte d'Arthur*.

trained: Royal Welsh College of Music and Drama.

theatre includes: *Six Characters in Search of an Author* (Chichester/West End); *Hamlet* (National Youth Theatre of Wales). Richard Burton Award winner 2004.

theatre whilst training includes: *The Comedy of Errors* (RSC Complete Works Festival), *The Winter's Tale, Twelfth Night, Gas, Take Me, Somewhere, Quadrophenia, The Crucible, The Seagull.*

television includes: *Caerdydd, Rownd & Rownd, Pen Tennyn, A470.*

film includes: *I Know You Know, The Baker, Oed yr Addewid.*

Phillip Edgerley

GUARD 1/ BREZHNEV

RSC: *The Two Gentlemen of Verona, Julius Caesar.*

Ensemble productions: Guard 1/Brezhnev in *Little Eagles*, Cleomenes in *The Winter's Tale*, Flavius/Popilius/Antony's Servant/Volumnius in *Julius Caesar*, 2nd Babitsky/Saveliev in *The Drunks*, Knight/Doctor/Curan in *King Lear*, Menas/Proculeius in *Antony and Cleopatra*.

trained: The London Centre for Theatre Studies, The Actors Company.

theatre includes: *Gone Too Far* (Royal Court); *Some Kinda Arizona* (Croydon Warehouse); *Julius Caesar* (Lyric Hammersmith); *Duck Variations, Kiss of*

the Spiderwoman, Mary Stuart, Hamlet* (Nuffield); *Much Ado about Nothing, Doctor Faustus* (Oxford Shakespeare Co.); *Luther* (National Theatre); *A Day Well Spent, On the Razzle* (Chichester Festival); *A Bed Full of Foreigners* (Theatre Royal); *Dancing at Lughnasa, Been So Long* (Jermyn Street); *Another Country* (Brockley Jack Theatre); *Bookworms, The Crucible, King Lear* (Fringe).

television includes: *Doctors, Life As We Know It, EastEnders, Footballers' Wives, Ultimate Force, The Bill.*

film includes: *Dead Rich, Chicane.*

radio includes: *Bernice Summerfield - The Empire State, Doctor Who: Time Works.*

Ti Green

DESIGNER

RSC: *Coriolanus* (RSC tour/Old Vic); *Julius Caesar* (tour).

this season: *Little Eagles.*

trained: Cambridge University and the Slade School of Art, London.

theatre includes: *The Overcoat* (Gecko/Lyric Hammersmith); *Liberty* (Shakespeare's Globe); *The Revenger's Tragedy, The Five Wives of Maurice Pinder, Coram Boy, The UN Inspector* (National Theatre); *The Resistible Rise of Arturo UI, The Ramayana* (Lyric Hammersmith); *King Cotton* (Lowry); *Coram Boy* (Imperial Theater, New York); *The*

Hound of the Baskervilles (West Yorkshire Playhouse/ Duchess); *Separate Tables* (Royal Exchange, Manchester); *Sante* (LSO/ St Lukes and Aldeburgh); *Tamburlaine* (Bristol Old Vic/ Barbican); *Compact Failure* (Cleanbreak); *Paradise Lost*, *The Comedy of Errors* (Bristol Old Vic); *The Entertainer* (Liverpool Everyman); *Food Chain* (Royal Court); *Dimetos*, *The Birds* (Gate); *Where There's a Will* (Theatre Royal Bath); *Full House*, *The Hairless Diva* (Watford Palace); *The Taming of the Shrew* (Nottingham Playhouse); *The Christmas Carol*, *Oedipus*, *Treasure Island*, *The Tempest*, *The Wind in the Willows*, *The John Wayne Principle*, *Twelfth Night* (Nuffield); *Bogus Woman* (Bush/Drum/national tour); *Dona Rosita*, *The Spinster*, *Macbeth*, *Bodies*, *Simpleton of the Unexpected Isles*, *Retreat* (Orange Tree).

Greg Hicks

OLD MAN/GELADZE

RSC: *Macbeth*, *Hamlet*, *Coriolanus*, *The Merry Wives of Windsor* (Old Vic/RSC), *Julius Caesar*, *Tantalus* (RSC/ Denver Centre), *Family Reunion*, *Romeo and Juliet*.
Ensemble productions: Old Man/Geladze in *Little Eagles*,

Leontes in *The Winter's Tale*, Julius Caesar in *Julius Caesar*, Tramp in *The Grain Store*, King Lear in *King Lear*, Soothsayer/ Thidias/Menecrates in *Antony and Cleopatra*.
trained: Rose Bruford.
theatre includes: *In Blood – The Bacchae*, *Small Craft Warnings*, *An Enemy of the People* (Arcola); *Don Quixote* (West Yorkshire Playhouse); *Angels in America* (Headlong/ Lyric Hammersmith); *The Lady of Leisure* (Liverpool Playhouse); *Missing Persons* (Trafalgar Studios/ Assembly Rooms); *Tamburlaine the Great* (TMA Award for Best Performance in a Play. Bristol Old Vic/ Barbican); *Messiah*, *King Lear*, *Waiting for Godot*, *The Seagull*, *Waste* (Old Vic); *The Bacchae*, *The Oedipus Plays* (and Greece), *Absolute Hell*, *The Cherry Orchard*, *The Duchess of Malfi*, *Coriolanus*, *Animal Farm*, *You Can't Take it with You*, *Lorenzaccio*, *Oresteia*, *The Spanish Tragedy* (National Theatre).
television includes: *Casualty*, *Trial and Retribution*, *Waking the Dead*, *Tiberius Gracchus*, *The Ten Commandments*, *Guardian*, *Jason and the Argonauts*.

James Howard

IVANOVSKY

Ensemble productions: Ivanovsky in *Little Eagles*, First Lord in *As You Like It*, 2nd Subordinate/Man in Hat in *The Drunks*, Paris in *Romeo and Juliet*, Ector/Bernard of Astolat/Lionel in *Morte d'Arthur*.
trained: Bristol Old Vic Theatre School.
theatre includes: *Twelfth Night*, *Ivanov* (Donmar Warehouse at Wyndham's); *The Revenger's Tragedy* (Southwark Playhouse); *Twelfth Night* (Northcott, Exeter); *Antony and Cleopatra* (Royal Exchange); *The Private Room* (New End); *The Duchess of Malfi*, *Lear* (National Theatre); *The Merchant of Venice* (Bristol Old Vic).
television includes: *Skins*, *Emmerdale*, *Midsomer Murders*, *The Bill*, *Natural Wonders*, *Spooks*, *Dream Team*, *The Inspector Lynley Mysteries*.
film includes: *The Oxford Murders*, *Penelope*, *Shoot on Sight*.
radio includes: *The Archers*, *The Last Country House*, *An Odd Body*, *Tarnished Wings*, *Protection*, *Bloody Stefi*, *Death of a Village*.

Ansu Kabia

KOMAROV

Ensemble productions:
Komarov in *Little Eagles*, Le Beau in *As You Like It*, Vasilii in *The Grain Store*, Duke of Burgundy/Herald in *King Lear*, Varrius in *Antony and Cleopatra*.

trained: Drama Centre, London.

theatre credits include:
Wedding Dance (national tour); *The Great Theatre of the World* (Arcola); *Romeo and Juliet* (Harlow Playhouse); *Rosencrantz and Guildenstern are Dead*, *Much Ado about Nothing* (Library Theatre, Manchester); *Blue/Orange* (Cockpit); *Othello* (Upstairs at the Gatehouse); *I'm an Asylum Seeker – Get Me Into Here* (Rosemary Branch); *Galileo* (C Venue, Edinburgh).

television includes: *The Bill*, *Casualty*, *10 Days to War*.

Stephen Kemble

COMPANY TEXT AND VOICE WORK

RSC: *Arabian Nights*, *The Tragedy of Thomas Hobbes*, *The Cordelia Dream*, *Dunsinane*. Stephen has also worked on the RSC's London seasons.

this season: *Little Eagles*.

trained: Voice Studies MA at Central School of Speech and Drama.

other work: Stephen's acting career has spanned more than 30 years and along with theatre, film and television, has included a huge amount of voiceover work. Text and voice coaching has subsequently become a significant part of his life working in theatre, actor training, and with individuals from all walks of life. He has a particular interest in voice for microphone and has helped develop voiceover training in several drama schools. His most recent accent and dialect work was on *Mary Broome*, currently at the Orange Tree Theatre.

Terry King

FIGHT DIRECTOR

RSC: Recent productions include: *Dunsinane*, *Othello*, *Hamlet*, *A Midsummer Night's Dream*, *The Histories Cycle*, *Noughts & Crosses*, *Antony and Cleopatra*, *Julius Caesar*, *King John*, *Pericles*, *The Indian Boy*, *Merry Wives the Musical*, *A Midsummer Night's Dream*, *Twelfth Night*, *As You Like It*, *Gunpowder Season*.

Ensemble productions:
Little Eagles, *As You Like It*, *The Drunks*, *The Grain Store*, *Hamlet*, *Romeo and Juliet*, *Antony and Cleopatra*.

trained: Bristol Old Vic Theatre School.

theatre includes: *The Lord of the Rings*, *On an Average Day*, *Ragtime*, *Chitty Chitty Bang Bang* (West End); *Accidental Death of an Anarchist*, *Caligula* (Donmar); *King Lear*, *The Murderers*, *Fool for Love*, *Duchess of Malfi*, *Henry V*, *Edmund*, *Jerry Springer the Opera* (National Theatre); *Oleanna*, *Search and Destroy*, *Sore Throats* (Royal Court).

opera includes: *Othello* (WNO); *Porgy and Bess* (Glyndebourne); *West Side Story* (York); *Carmen* (ENO).

television includes: *Fell Tiger*, *A Kind of Innocence*, *A Fatal Inversion*, *The Bill*, *EastEnders*, *Measure for Measure*, *Casualty*, *The Widowing of Mrs. Holroyd*, *Death of a Salesman*.

Debbie Korley

RITA/NATASHA

Ensemble productions:
Rita/Natasha in *Little Eagles*, Hisperia in *As You Like It*, Luciana in *The Comedy of Errors*, Gafiika in *The Grain Store*, Ophelia/Player/Pirate in *Hamlet*, Lady in *Romeo and Juliet*, Nimue in *Morte d'Arthur*.

theatre includes: *Coram Boy*, *A Matter of Life and Death* (National Theatre); *Feathers in the Snow* (National Theatre Studio); *Cinderella* (Theatre Royal, Stratford East);

Whistle Down the Wind (West End/tour); *Sick!* (Almeida); *Ten Suitcases* (Drill Hall); *Aida* (Royal Albert Hall); *Carmen Jones* (Old Vic); *The Vagina Monologues* (Mercury, Colchester); *Saturday Night* (White Bear); *Annie* (Edinburgh Festival/National Youth Music Theatre).

television includes: *Doctors, Casualty, Holy Smoke, Night and Day, Green Balloon Club*.

Helen Leblique

ASSISTANT DIRECTOR

Ensemble productions: *Little Eagles, The Winter's Tale, The Drunks, Antony and Cleopatra*.

theatre includes: As Director: *Up the Duff* (rehearsed reading); *Trifles, Playgoers, The Twelve Pound Look* (Orange Tree); *A Hitch in Time* (Exeter Northcott, New Writing Festival); *Othello* (Roborough Studio). As Assistant Director: *Far from the Madding Crowd* (English Touring Theatre); *War and Peace* (Shared Experience); *The Madras House, Major Barbara, The Pirates of Penzance, Nan* (Orange Tree); *Hysteria* (Exeter Northcott).

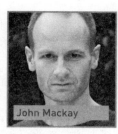

John Mackay

GLUSHKO/STEVE

RSC: *The Histories Cycle, Twelfth Night, As You Like It, Pilate, Hamlet, Macbeth*.

Ensemble productions: Glushko/Steve in *Little Eagles*, Camillo in *The Winter's Tale*, Cassius in *Julius Caesar*, Mortko in *The Grain Store*, Duke of Albany in *King Lear*, Caesar in *Antony and Cleopatra*.

trained: Bristol Old Vic Theatre School.

theatre includes: *Six Characters in Search of an Author* (Headlong/West End); *Dark Earth* (Traverse); *All My Sons* (York Theatre Royal); *War Music* (Sound and Fury); *Troilus and Cressida, As You Like It, The Winter's Tale, Twelfth Night, Coriolanus, Measure for Measure, A Midsummer Night's Dream, King Lear* (Shakespeare at the Tobacco Factory).

television includes: *Law and Order UK, Doc Martin, Trial and Retribution, Casualty, London's Burning*.

radio includes: *Heart of Darkness, Night and Day, Madeleine, Soldier Soldier, Evelina, The Iliad, Poetry Please*.

Rona Munro

WRITER

RSC: *The Indian Boy*.

this season: *Little Eagles*.

Rona has written extensively for stage, radio, film and television including the award winning plays *Iron, Bold Girls* and *The Maiden Stone*. Other plays include *The Last Witch* for the Edinburgh International Festival, *Long Time Dead* produced by Paines Plough and adaptations of *Mary Barton* and *Watership Down* which were produced by Manchester Royal Exchange and the Lyric Hammersmith. Film and telvision work includes: the Ken Loach film *Ladybird Ladybird, Aimee And Jaguar* and TV dramas *Rehab* and BAFTA nominated *Bumping The Odds* for the BBC. She has also written many other single plays for radio and television and contributed to series such as *Casualty* and *Doctor Who*. She is the co-founder and resident writer for Scotland's most successful small scale touring theatre company, The MsFits whose most recent production, *Mad Bad and Dangerous to Know*, began a tour throughout the UK in March 2011. Her play *Pandas* opened at the Traverse Theatre, Edinburgh in April 2011. She also wrote the screenplay for the film *Oranges And Sunshine* directed by Jim Loach and starring Emily Watson which went on general release in April 2011.

Sandy Neilson

Peter Peverley

STALIN/YAKOV

RSC: *The Histories Cycle*.
Ensemble productions:
Stalin/Yakov in *Little Eagles*,
Duke Frederick in *As You Like It*, Babitsky in *The Drunks*,
Knight in *King Lear*, Lepidus in *Antony and Cleopatra*.
trained: RSAMD.
theatre includes: *Realism*
(National Theatre of Scotland);
Tales from Hollywood (Perth Theatre); *Cyprus* (Trafalgar Studios/Mull Theatre);
Macbeth (Theatre Babel);
Death of a Salesman
(Edinburgh Lyceum); *Ghosts*
(Belfast Lyric); *Too Late for Logic* (Edinburgh International Festival); *The Duchess of Malfi*, *The Winter's Tale*, *A Midsummer Night's Dream*,
Dancing at Lughnasa (Dundee Theatre).
television includes: *Mr Hyde*, *Secret of the Stars*, *Still Game*, *Cathedral*, *Taggart*:
Penthouse and Pavement,
The Greeks, *Mr Wymi*, *The 39 Steps*.
film includes: *Young Adam*,
A Shot at Glory, *The Debt Collector*, *The Winter Guest*.

MISHIN

Ensemble productions:
Mishin in *Little Eagles*,
Jaques De Boys/Dennis in
As You Like It, Balthazar in
The Comedy of Errors, Young Kostya/1st Barfly in *The Drunks*, Polonius/1st Sailor/ Priest/Pirate in *Hamlet*, Friar John/Abraham/Watchman in *Romeo and Juliet*, Mordred in *Morte d'Arthur*.
trained: Newcastle College.
theatre includes: *Twelfth Night*, *Threepenny Opera*,
Great Expectations, *Animal Farm*, *Clockwork Orange*,
Grimm's Tales, *The Ballroom of Romance*, *Elmer McCurdy Rides Again*, *Pinocchio*,
Edmund, *The Dumb Waiter*,
Glengarry Glen Ross, *The Long Line*, *Andorra*, *The Snow Queen*, *Son of Man*
(Northern Stage Ensemble 1998-2006); *The Firework-Maker's Daughter* (Told by an Idiot/Sheffield Crucible);
The Venetian Twins (Octagon, Bolton); *Greenfingers* (Live Theatre/Northern Stage)
Cabaret, *Oh! What a Lovely War* (Live Theatre, Newcastle);
Beautiful Game (Theatre Royal Newcastle); *Get Off at Gateshead* (Gala, Durham);
Accounts (Northumberland Theatre Co.); *Much Ado about*

Nothing (Mad Alice Theatre Co.); *The Little Waster* (one man show).
television includes: *Byker Grove*, *Emmerdale*, *Harry*, *Spender*, *The Parables*.
writing: The Little Waster.
composition includes: *The Golden Bird*, *Black Eyed Roses* (Northern Stage).

MUSIC AND SOUND DESIGN

RSC debut season: *Little Eagles*.
other theatre includes:
Racing Demon (Sheffield Crucible); *Les Parents Terrible* (Donmar at Trafalgar Studios); *Electric Hotel*
(Sadler's Wells/Fuel); *Hamlet*
(Sheffield Crucible); *Salome*
(Headlong); *The Man from Stratford* (Ambassadors);
Polar Bears (Donmar); *The Little Dog Laughed* (Garrick);
Three Days of Rain (Apollo, West End); *The Rise and Fall of Little Voice* (Vaudeville);
The Author (Royal Court); *The Pride* (Royal Court); *An Enemy of the People* (Sheffield Crucible); *Really Old Like Forty Five* (National); Phaedra (Donmar); *Piaf* (Donmar/ Vaudeville/Buenos Aires);
Branded, *All About my Mother* (Old Vic); *Contains Violence* (Lyric Hammersmith);
The Lover/The Collection (Comedy, West End); *The Caretaker* (Sheffield Crucible/ Tricycle/tour); *Amato Saltone*,
What If…? Tropicana, *Dance Bear Dance*, *The Ballad of*

Bobby Francois (Shunt); *The Pigeon* (BAC); *Henry IV Parts I and II* (National Theatre). Ben and Max won Best Overall Achievement in an Affiliate Theatre Olivier award for *The Pride*.

other work includes: Ben and Max are associate artists with the Shunt collective and two thirds of the band Superthriller.

Oliver Ryan

LEONOV

Ensemble productions: Leonov in *Little Eagles*, Servant in *The Winter's Tale*, Casca/Pindarus in *Julius Caesar*, Gorobets in *The Grain Store*, Benvolio in *Romeo and Juliet*, Gawain in *Morte d'Arthur*.

theatre includes: *Memory* (Clwyd Theatr Cymru/ The Pleasance, New York); *Macbeth, Arcadia, One Flew Over the Cuckoo's Nest, The Crucible, Rosencrantz and Guildenstern are Dead, The Rabbit, King Lear, Of Mice and Men, Afore Night Come, Equus* (Clwyd Theatr Cymru); *Nostalgia* (Plymouth Drum); *Richard II, Coriolanus* (Almeida/New York/Tokyo); *Unprotected Sex, Everything Must Go* (Sherman Theatre); *Hamlet* (Birmingham Rep).

television includes: *Casualty, Midsomer Murders, Doctors, A Harlot's Progress, High Hopes, The Bill, Life and Debt, The Bench, A Mind to Kill, Holby City, Jack of Hearts.*
film: *Killing Me Softly.*

Roxana Silbert

DIRECTOR

RSC: Associate Director. *Dunsinane, Brixton Stories.*
this season: *Little Eagles.*
Roxana was previously Artistic Director of Paines Plough (2005-2009), Literary Director at Traverse Theatre (2001-2004), Associate Director at Royal Court (1999-2001) and Trainee Associate Director at West Yorkshire Playhouse (1998-1999).

theatre includes: *Orphans, Roaring Trade* (Paines Plough); *Being Norwegian, Between Wolf and Dog* (Paines Plough/Oran Mor); *Long Time Dead* (Paines Plough/ Plymouth Theatre Royal/Traverse); *Strawberries in January* (Paines Plough/ Traverse); *Under the Black Flag* (Shakespeare's Globe); *After the End* (Paines Plough/ Traverse/ Bush/59e59/ international tour); *Dallas Sweetman* (Canterbury Cathedral); *Whistle in the Dark* (Citizen's Theatre); *Precious, Blond Bombshells* (West Yorkshire Playhouse); *Property* (National Theatre Studio); *Damages* (Bush); *The Slab Boys, Still Life from the Slab Boys Trilogy* (Traverse/national tour); *The People Next Door*

(Traverse/Theatre Royal, Stratford East); *Iron* (Traverse/ Royal Court); *15 Seconds, Greenfields* (Traverse); *The Price* (Bolton Octagon); *Top Girls, Translations* (New Vic, Stoke); *Cadillac Ranch* (Soho); *At the Table, Still Nothing, I Was So Lucky, Been So Long, Fairgame, Bazaar, Sweetheart* (Royal Court); *Mules* (Royal Court/Clean Break Theatre Co./national tour); *Slash Hatch on the E* (Donmar).

radio includes: *Hysteria, Billiards, Japanese Gothic Tales, The Tall One, The Tape Recorded Highlights of a Humble Bee, The Good Father, Brace Position.*

Ayse Tashkiran

MOVEMENT DIRECTOR

RSC: *The God's Weep, Days of Significance.*
this season: *Little Eagles.*
trained: Bristol University and Lecoq, Paris.

theatre includes: *The Chairs* (Bath Theatre Royal); *Sweeney Todd* (Welsh National Opera MAX); *Chi Chi Bunichi* (tour); *Feast on the Bridge* (Thames Festival); *Sarajevo Story* (Lyric Hammersmith); *Silent Tide, Forget Me Not* (London International Mime Festival); *Ma Vie en Rose* (Young Vic); *Macbeth* (Regent's Park); *Stacy* (Trafalgar Studios); *La Songe du 21 Juin* (national tour/France); *Brixton Stories* (Lyric Hammersmith Studio); *The Beggar's Opera*

(Blackheath Concert Hall); *Orfeo* (Greenwich); *All's Well that Ends Well* (Young Vic, Young Directors Scheme); *Here's What I Did with my Body One Day* (national tour/ Pleasance).

Chahine Yavroyan

LIGHTING DESIGNER

RSC: *Dunsinane*, *God in Ruins*.
this season: *Little Eagles*.
recent theatre includes: *Bronte* (Shared Experience); *Scorched* (Old Vic Tunnels); *Dr Marigold & Mr Chops* (Riverside); *1984* (Blind Summit at BAC); *Orphans* (Paines Plough/Soho); *Fuente Ovejuna ll Castigo Sin Vengansa* (Madrid); *Damascus* (Traverse/Tricycle/ Middle East); *Relocated*, *Wig Out!*, *Get Santa* (Royal Court); *Three Sisters*, *Comedy of Errors*, *The Lady from the Sea* (Royal Exchange); *Dallas Sweetman* (Paines Plough/ Canterbury Cathedral); *Sun & Heir* (Royal Opera House/ Tilbury Cruise Terminal); *Fall* (Traverse); *Il Tempo Del Postino* (MIF/Manchester Opera House); *The Wonderful World of Dissocia* (National Theatre of Scotland/Royal Court); *Long Time Dead* (Paines Plough/Drum/ Traverse).
other work includes: Recent dance work with Jasmin Vardimon, Frauke Requardt, Arthur Pita, CanDoCo, Bock & Vincenzi. Music work: *Diamanda*

Galas (international); *Dalston Songs* (ROH2); *Plague Songs* (Barbican Hall). Site specific work: *Fables* (Streetwise Opera); *Ghost Sonata* (The People Show/Sefton Park Plamhouse); *Light Touch*, *Dedicated*, *Focal Point for Scarabeus*, *Enchanted Parks*, *Spa*, *Deep End for Corridor*.

Hannah Young

ANNA/XENIA

RSC: *The Merry Wives of Windsor*, *Coriolanus* (RSC/ Old Vic), *The Lion, the Witch and the Wardrobe* (Sadler's Wells).
Ensemble productions: Anna/Xenia in *Little Eagles*, Emilia in *The Winter's Tale*, Portia in *Julius Caesar*, Natasha in *The Drunks*, Nurse in *King Lear*, Charmian in *Antony and Cleopatra*.
trained: University of Exeter.
theatre includes: *Corporate Rock* (Nabokov); *The Lady from the Sea* (Birmingham Rep); *Songs of Grace and Redemption* (Theatre503); *The French Lieutenant's Woman* (Yvonne Arnaud/No.1 tour); *As You Desire* (Playhouse, West End); *Time and the Conways* (Theatre Royal Bath/No.1 tour); *First Love*, Kishon Brook (International Playwrighting Festival,

Royal Court); *A Chaste Maid in Cheapside* (Almeida/ No.1 tour); *Les Liaisons Dangereuses* (Liverpool Playhouse); *A Midsummer Night's Dream* (Albery, West End); *The Importance of Being Earnest* (Deptford Albany); *Queer Dorset Bastard* (Camden Etcetera); *The Stringless Marionette* (Orange Tree); *The Swell* (Theatre Alibi).
television includes: *Britain's Nazi King*, *Doctors*, *The Robinsons*, *Waking the Dead*, *Offenders*.
film: *Alan's Breakfast*.
radio: *Levitt in London*.

Samantha Young

VALYA

RSC: *I'll be the Devil*.
Ensemble productions:
Valya in *Little Eagles*,
Perdita in *The Winter's Tale*,
Soothsayer's Acolyte in *Julius Caesar*, Mokrina Staritskaya
in *The Grain Store*, Cordelia in
King Lear, Iras in *Antony and Cleopatra*.
trained: RSAMD.
theatre includes: *Videotape*
(Oran Mor); *Fall* (Traverse,
Edinburgh); *Hamlet* (Glasgow
Citizens); *Europe* (Dundee
Rep/Barbican); *Gobbo*, *Miss Julie*, *The Crucible* (National
Theatre of Scotland); *A Taste of Honey* (Glasgow Citizens);
The Graduate, *The Visit*,
A Lie of the Mind, *Macbeth*
(Dundee Rep); *Snow White*
(Glasgow Citizens).
television includes:
Casualty, *River City*.
short film: *Mono*.
radio includes: *Freefalling*,
Look Back in Anger, *Almost Blue*.

JOIN US

Join us from £18 a year.

Join today and make a difference

The Royal Shakespeare Company is an ensemble. We perform all year round in our Stratford-upon-Avon home, as well as having regular seasons in London, and touring extensively within the UK and overseas for international residencies.

With a range of options from £18 to £10,000 per year, there are many ways to engage with the RSC.

Choose a level that suits you and enjoy a closer connection with us whilst also supporting our work on stage.

Find us online

Sign up for regular email updates at **www.rsc.org.uk/signup**

Join today

Annual RSC Full Membership costs just £40 (or £18 for Associate Membership) and provides you with regular updates on RSC news, advance information and priority booking.

Support us

A charitable donation from £100 a year can offer you the benefits of membership, whilst also allowing you the opportunity to deepen your relationship with the Company through special events, backstage tours and exclusive ticket booking services.

The options include Shakespeare's Circle (from £100), Patrons' Circle (Silver: £1,000, Gold: £5,000) and Artists' Circle (£10,000).

For more information visit **www.rsc.org.uk/joinus** or call the RSC Membership Office on 01789 403 440.

Hampstead Theatre is one of the UK's leading new writing companies – a company that has just celebrated its fiftieth year of operation.

Throughout its long history the theatre has existed to support a thriving local, national and international playwriting culture. We commission plays in order to enrich and enliven this culture. We support, develop and produce the work of new writers, emerging writers, established writers, mid-career writers and senior writers and have a proud tradition for creating the conditions for their plays and careers to develop.

The list of playwrights who had their early work produced at Hampstead Theatre and who are now filling theatres all over the country and beyond include Mike Leigh, Michael Frayn, Brian Friel, Terry Johnson, Hanif Kureishi, Simon Block, Abi Morgan, Rona Munro, Tamsin Oglesby, Harold Pinter, Shelagh Stephenson, debbie tucker green, Crispin Whittell, Roy Williams and Dennis Kelly.

The Creative Learning programme is also an integral part of Hampstead Theatre's work. We aim to celebrate all aspects of the creative process in ways which support learning and widen access to the theatre's programme. Inspiring creativity and developing emerging talent, at its best our work has the power to change lives.

In January 2010, Edward Hall was appointed Artistic Director of Hampstead Theatre. Hall's inaugural season was a box office success culminating in a West End transfer of Mike Leigh's revival of *Ecstasy*. Hampstead Theatre looks forward to welcoming the RSC and Hall's own company, the internationally acclaimed Propeller, over the forthcoming months.

Hampstead Downstairs was opened in November 2010. It seats 98 and stages raw, edgy and experimental work. The audience decide for themselves what they think of the work, with their decisions not being predetermined by media reviews. Previous productions include *small hours* directed by Katie Mitchell and *.45* written by Gary Lennon.

Hall's second season, autumn 2011, will continue to delight, inspire and engage with such directors as Katie Mitchell, Richard Eyre and Roger Michell taking to the stage.

Hampstead Theatre, Eton Avenue, Swiss Cottage, London NW3 3EU

www.hampsteadtheatre.com

Registered charity number: 218506

LITTLE EAGLES

Rona Munro

For all the wonderful, welcoming people at Davidson College, North Carolina without whom the rocket would never have got off the launch pad

Author's Note

Little Eagles is intended as the first part of a trilogy of plays about the years of space exploration that formed such a significant backdrop to my childhood. Like many others of my age I still can't quite believe that the astronauts and cosmonauts I thought would be part of our future have instead become part of our history.

I only encountered the extraordinary story of the mysterious Chief Designer after I began my research and it quickly muscled its way into the centre of this narrative.

Writing any play based on real events and characters is a daunting exercise. In writing about Sergei Pavlovich Korolyov and the others who inhabit this play, I have had to take some glaring liberties with time and space and imagined events and emotions which may never have occurred or, if they did, may not have occurred as I've chosen to portray them. I've invented some characters, condensed others and turned great chunks of detailed human history into a few short scenes. I don't think I'd have been doing my job if I hadn't dared to mess things around like this, it was a very necessary outcome to the wonderful wrestling match any writer goes through turning real events (in this case on an epic scale) into drama. However, if I've offended the better informed amongst you, rocket scientists, historians, space enthusiasts, with some of my choices I sincerely hope it won't detract from your enjoyment of the story.

I should also ask forgiveness of the dead and the indulgence of the living, some of whom have been fictionalised in our play. I hope they will agree that this incredible story and this incredible character deserve wider exposure and any liberties are excusable. If there's any justice, this will be far from the last version of these events an audience may enjoy.

Those who are interested can seek out the same research material I did – thank God for the world wide web and for some very well-written academic and popular science and history books about this fascinating period. There they will discover that while they might not always agree with my interpretation of events (and there will always be as many interpretations as there are subjective viewpoints), I have not exaggerated either the achievements or the genius of the Chief Designer or the early successes of the Soviet scientists who pushed humanity out of the Earth's atmosphere.

Rona Munro

This text went to press before the end of rehearsals and so may differ slightly from the play as performed.

Characters

STALIN
KOROLYOV
OLD MAN
GUARD ONE
GUARD TWO
CONDEMNED MAN
DOCTOR
XENIA
NATASHA
GLUSHKO
MISHIN
IVANOVSKY
KHRUSHCHEV
BREZHNEV
GULAG WORKER
YURI GAGARIN
VALYA
KOMAROV
TITOV
OFFICER
GULAG PRISONER
GENERAL GELADZE
TECHNICIAN
GUINEA PIG
ANNA
RITA
YAKOV
FARMER
ENGINEER
STEVE

SCHIRRA, STAFFORD, BORMAN, LOVELL *and* MISSION CONTROL (*voiceovers*)

And GULAG WORKERS, DESIGN ENGINEERS, GUARDS, MEMBERS OF THE POLITBURO

ACT ONE

Scene One

Kolyma Gulag, 1938.

STALIN *stands high above the frozen steppes.*

STALIN. Comrades.

Our country is attacked from within. Only the most naive among you can doubt that our enemies are right in the heart of our great nation, like rats in a barrel of wheat. We all know that the agents of all the bourgeois countries prey upon each other, sewing war and creating discord inside each other's borders. We know too that these same bourgeois countries consider us, the Soviet people, to be their greatest enemy. Of course they have sent their agents, their spies among us. Who can doubt it?

And even as we struggle against this foreign disease we still have failed to root out every germ of our own illnesses, Trotskyites and other double-dealers are living amongst us.

As STALIN *speaks, the* GULAG WORKERS *enter one by one. The Gulag is a frozen wasteland, an icy, open-cast gold mine. It's just after sunset. The* GULAG WORKERS *are scraping at the icy earth. They are all sick, very weak.*

Some have accused our loyal agents of using excessive physical pressure against those who have been arrested. Some have even said that these faithful comrades have behaved like criminals themselves. But a party directive, made in 1937, indicated such force could be used in exceptional cases. I ask those who criticise this action to tell us how otherwise we are to defend ourselves against blatant enemies of the people. Enemies who, when interrogated by humane methods, defiantly refuse to turn over the names of co-conspirators. Enemies who refuse for months on end to provide any evidence. Enemies who try to thwart the unmasking of co-conspirators still at large, and who thereby continue, even from prison, to wage a struggle against the Soviet regime. The use of force requires courage but our experience has taught us no other method can produce results. The defence of the Soviet people demands all our strength.

There is no other case to answer.

What is done is done by the will of the people as all their actions demonstrate.

STALIN *exits but his presence remains onstage in some visible form.*

One by one the GULAG PRISONERS *stop working, some collapsing altogether, others struggling to continue.*

One of them, KOROLYOV, *looks up at the sky. He smiles. The worker beside him, an* OLD MAN, *sees him.*

OLD MAN. Who's up there?

KOROLYOV. Venus. The evening star. Close and bright in the blue dusk. You can see the shape of her.

OLD MAN. You got a biscuit, comrade?

KOROLYOV. What?

OLD MAN. They fed you, there was none left for an old man, I couldn't reach it in time. Were there biscuits? I'll lick the crumbs off your fingers, comrade, anything.

Something sweet. I'd give my soul for something sweet on my tongue, comrade.

KOROLYOV. There's never any biscuits, you old fool.

I've nothing.

Two GUARDS *drag on another* WORKER; *an execution. They position him and then aim their guns. The* DOCTOR *follows them on.*

DOCTOR. Wait...! I didn't mean...

The CONDEMNED MAN *raises his arms to* STALIN.

CONDEMNED MAN. Long live Comrade Stalin!

GUARD ONE (*meaning it*). Well said, comrade!

They shoot him.

They turn to the DOCTOR. *The* DOCTOR *is in her late twenties. She has never seen anyone shot before.*

You were saying.

DOCTOR. I didn't mean... I didn't mean...

GUARD TWO. You said he was dead.

DOCTOR. I didn't mean...

GUARD ONE. You said he was as good as dead already.

DOCTOR. I didn't...!

GUARD TWO. You said,

(*Looks at notes.*) 'If he's under sentence of death you might as well shoot him now and get it over with...'

GUARD ONE. '...it'd be kinder.'

That's what you said.

GUARD TWO. And he was under sentence of death. So we did.

GUARD ONE (*pushing paperwork at her*). Sign.

GUARD TWO. We did your kindness for you.

GUARD ONE. Sign.

GUARD TWO. Put your name to it. Put your name to your recommendation, as medical officer in charge.

GUARD ONE. Go on, sign.

They're closing in on the DOCTOR, *intimidating her.*

GUARD TWO. Sign it!

GUARD ONE. Put your name on the paper, comrade!

KOROLYOV (*to the* DOCTOR). They can't make you do that.

DOCTOR. What?

KOROLYOV. Someone needs to be responsible, for the paperwork, death must be recorded, execution quotas must be precise, they've acted without paperwork...

GUARD ONE *silences him. A vicious blow.*

GUARD TWO. Sign.

The DOCTOR *signs.*

DOCTOR. What I said… What I meant… there is only enough medicine to treat one person… I only have enough to save one of them… but no one should die from this disease, no one deserves that death… it's too cruel…

GUARD ONE. So treat them.

DOCTOR. I only have enough for one person!

GUARD TWO. So pick one!

DOCTOR. We have to requisition supplies! I need you to contact your superior officers and tell them we need more supplies!

GUARD ONE (*to* GUARD TWO). When did she get here?

GUARD TWO. I'm guessing yesterday.

GUARD ONE (*to* DOCTOR). You are the last new, clean and healthy thing whose feet will break the dirty snow here till next May. No drugs. No daylight. No escape…

(*Moving in on her.*) Nothing else sweet and soft and fresh for a thousand miles…

DOCTOR. Stay away from me! I'll report you, comrade.

GUARD ONE. I don't think so, it's a long way to Moscow, sweetheart.

GUARD TWO (*warning*). Pieter Nikolyavich…

GUARD ONE. Pick one and save his life. Just make sure it's worth saving.

GUARD TWO. Yeah, the bastards have got to be able to work, that's why they're here.

GUARD ONE (*calling out to* GULAG WORKERS). Hey! We've got one dose of the life-saving shit that'll stop you shitting your souls out your arse. One dose for a worker. Who's fit to work?

Some of the GULAG WORKERS *call out, stumbling to their feet.*

Well, will you look at that? It's a medical miracle, they have all made a miraculous recovery!

(*To* GUARD TWO.) Move them out to break the new site.

GUARD TWO. Move.

Starts pushing the GULAG WORKERS *out, clearing away the dead body.*

GUARD ONE. Pick one. Make sure he's worth saving. You're the angel of life and death. Enjoy.

DOCTOR. You have the fever already.

The DOCTOR *is left with* KOROLYOV, *the* OLD MAN *and another* GULAG WORKER. *It is bitter cold. Only* KOROLYOV *is fit to speak, the other two are far gone. The* DOCTOR *looks at the* OLD MAN. *Checks his pulse.*

You look like my father.

Moves to KOROLYOV. *Checks his pulse.*

What's your name, comrade?

KOROLYOV. Sergei Pavlovich Korolyov.

DOCTOR. What did you do, Sergei? Before they sent you here?

KOROLYOV. I… made… I flew…

I made… rockets… rockets.

DOCTOR. Fireworks or bombs?

KOROLYOV. To fly… we flew… I can't remember…

Let me live…

DOCTOR. Your heart's weak. They've cracked your ribs…

KOROLYOV. Help me, let me live, help me.

DOCTOR. Lie still, you're bleeding.

KOROLYOV. Help me see the sky…

DOCTOR. Careful… alright… gently…

She helps him. He looks up at the sky.

(*Treating his wounds.*) I've been posted here indefinitely. What does that mean? How long do doctors work here?

KOROLYOV. I don't know. A long time.

DOCTOR. I can't stay here.

KOROLYOV. I could have flown us both out of here.

DOCTOR. On a rocket.

KOROLYOV. Beyond the edge of the air, out into the sparkling dark and out of the reach of gravity... to the other side of the Moon. We would fly on forever.

DOCTOR. Good. Dream of that.

KOROLYOV. It's not a dream. It's not. I could do that.

DOCTOR. Not today you can't.

(*Starting to crack.*) How will I live here?

KOROLYOV. You breathe.

Don't cry.

DOCTOR. I'm not... I...

KOROLYOV. No. You have to stop. You have to stop crying if you want to live. One day you'll work somewhere else again. Keep thinking that. You'll escape.

DOCTOR. I don't deserve escape.

KOROLYOV. That's got nothing to do with it, comrade.

DOCTOR. No... No! I'm an idiot and a whore! He was a General. He promised me an apartment. Oh God, I so wanted an apartment! I thought I could suffer a few wet kisses, a few sweaty gropes...

I couldn't do it twice! I couldn't bear it when he came back for more. So he knew, it wasn't maidenly virtue, was it? He knew he made me heave. I couldn't hide it. I'm here because I'm only half a slut, only half a liar. If I knew how to be properly wicked I'd be safe by a stove in Spiridonovka.

I wanted a apartment! That's all! A window sill with sun on it! A pot of flowers. A cat. My own little bed with fresh sheets and someone pretty lying under them now and then. What's so wrong with that!? Why am I punished for that… Why am I here? I… Please… please… I didn't do anything wrong. I don't want to be here. I don't… I can't… I want to go home… I want a home…! I want a yellow painted wall and a kettle!

She gets herself together. She opens her medical bag and gets a needle ready.

I'm so sorry. I'm so sorry. I don't know what to do, Sergei Pavlovich.

KOROLYOV. Give it to him.

DOCTOR. He's old. He's barely breathing.

KOROLYOV (*the other worker*). Then give it to him.

DOCTOR. The fever's high in him already.

KOROLYOV. Then give it to me! Just do it!

DOCTOR. Promise me you're not a traitor, comrade.

Promise me you'll do no more harm.

KOROLYOV. I'm a man! If I'm alive I'll do harm!

DOCTOR. Then say you forgive me!

KOROLYOV. For what?

DOCTOR. For choosing who lives and who dies.

KOROLYOV. Fuck you, witch. You've got fur-lined boots.

The DOCTOR *pulls away from him. She goes to inject the* OLD MAN *but at the last moment turns back and gives* KOROLYOV *the life-saving vaccine.*

DOCTOR. You rotting traitor. Live then, for all the good it'll do you. You owe me one, Sergei Pavlovich.

The DOCTOR *exits.*

KOROLYOV. Witch.

The OLD MAN *groans.* KOROLYOV *struggles to him.*

OLD MAN. Is it time to go in? Help me in, son, I'll die out here.

KOROLYOV. I can't.

OLD MAN. Oh…

Oh… that's a fucker then…

KOROLYOV. Here.

He gives something to the OLD MAN.

OLD MAN. Sugar!

KOROLYOV. She had a lump in her pocket. I lifted it.

OLD MAN. The last sweet thing in Kolyma Gulag. You've been a good apprentice, Sergei Pavlovich. My time's not been wasted. You came here an enemy of the people and I've made an honest thief out of you. Did they hurt you?

KOROLYOV. I'll live.

OLD MAN. See that you do. One day you might go south again, eh? Make something of yourself. Live a bit of life for me.

KOROLYOV. I'll build a rocket… I'll send your fame all over the sky. 'The last honest thief' – you can steal a piece of the Moon.

OLD MAN. A rocket?

A rocket is no memorial is it, Sergei?

Sergei Pavlovich, you know full well all I wanted was another sugar lump.

Dip it in vodka, melt it on your tongue, then drain the rest and think of me.

What a fucking waste.

KOROLYOV. Hold onto me, comrade. Just hold on.

OLD MAN. You're right…

This isn't the time. I'm feeling lucky.

I could steal my own soul back from death if I put my mind to it.

But they tell me men have no souls these days.

You know who the devil is, Sergei?

KOROLYOV. Who?

OLD MAN (*laughing*). A bad boy from Smolensk, just like me.

Oh, look at that night...

So much ice in the air even the stars are shivering with it.

KOROLYOV. Hold on. You'll be alright.

OLD MAN. If you say so, son. Just don't forget me, eh?

KOROLYOV. Never.

OLD MAN. Good. That's good.

The OLD MAN *dies.*

Time passes. The night passes. The sun is coming up.
KOROLYOV *still sits with the frozen corpse of the*
OLD MAN.

GUARD TWO *enters. He has some papers in his hand.*

GUARD TWO. Sergei Pavlovich Korolyov...

KOROLYOV *says nothing.*

They want you in Moscow.

Holds up papers.

Official release for reassignment of labour. They want him to
stop breaking ice and rock and sit by a stove somewhere
doing sums...

I'm not joking.

Alright, I might be joking. I might just be waiting for the poor
fucker to stick his hand up so I can shoot the traitor in the
head. We'll never know unless he takes a gamble, will we...

KOROLYOV (*cuts him off*). I'm Korolyov.

The GUARD *raises his gun. Then he roars with laughter as*
KOROLYOV *flinches and drops the papers beside him.*

GUARD TWO. Better get yourself to Moscow, comrade.

KOROLYOV *struggles up. He just looks at the* GUARD,
dazed and confused.

What? You thought they'd send you a car? Better get walking, comrade. Only nine thousand kilometres to go.

KOROLYOV *turns to face the rising sun. He starts to walk towards it, blinded by the light, stumbling, freezing.*

Behind him the GULAG WORKERS *enter and are labouring again. Some of them drag the body of the* OLD MAN *offstage.*

KOROLYOV *keeps walking. He doesn't look back.*

Scene Two

The DESIGN ENGINEERS' *room.*

XENIA, NATASHA *and* GLUSHKO *come on,* XENIA *and* NATASHA *looking round at their unfamiliar surroundings.*

NATASHA. Why are we here?

GLUSHKO. This is where your father works, Natasha…

XENIA. Why are we here? Why haven't we been taken to the visiting room?

GLUSHKO. I'll explain. In a minute.

Is it what you imagined, Natasha?

NATASHA (*looking round*). No. This bit doesn't look like a prison.

GLUSHKO. Natasha Kuralyeva, you know this isn't really a prison, your father is working for his country…

XENIA. He's still a zek, there are guards, he's under lock and key. He's a prisoner. Why are we in here?

GLUSHKO. Sergei Pavlovich has a busy day today. It wouldn't be possible for him to stop work and see you today. So. I've brought you to him.

XENIA. He asked for us to come in here?

GLUSHKO. I'll explain. One of my assistants will give you a tour. We'll show you the living quarters, the kitchens, the dormitories... there's a very pretty wood... just beyond the fence... do you see? I don't suppose you've had time to explore it, Natasha, would you like to?

XENIA. Comrade Glushko, we've been on a train for three days. Am I to be permitted to see my husband?

GLUSHKO. This is a very important day, for the whole programme. I want you to know that I will do everything I can to ensure Sergei Pavolvich's pardon... We'll give you a tour. We'll show you the family apartments.

XENIA. Family apartments?

GLUSHKO. For employees of course, rather than the prisoners but... Well, I'm certain I can obtain you permission to occupy one. Almost definitely.

XENIA. What are you talking about?

GLUSHKO. You could see him... every day. And in time... if all goes well, if he's free... he could live with you. Everything would be as it was.

XENIA. We have an apartment. In Moscow. Why are you offering us an apartment here?

GLUSHKO. I need you to talk to Sergei. I need you to explain the advantages, to all of us, of success here today. You can see the advantages, Xenia...

XENIA. Why can't you talk to him?

I don't understand, Comrade Glushko, you've known him since you were students. You've worked together for nearly twenty years...

GLUSHKO. Not quite. No. We weren't able to work together, for many years, and I regret that, I want you... I want Sergei to understand, at last, how much I regret that...

Pause.

XENIA (*gets it*). Ah. This is why he hates you.

GLUSHKO. Sergei and I have...

XENIA (*interrupts*). You kept your job.

GLUSHKO. Yes, but...

XENIA. You kept your job. You have an apartment... You walk around under the sky, free to turn your face up to the sun or the snow, any time you like...

...you denounced him. Didn't you, Comrade Glushko?

Pause.

GLUSHKO. Look, you don't have much time, Xenia, I thought you would have arrived yesterday...

XENIA (*interrupts*). You denounced him. You sent him to the Gulag.

And now you're his boss.

(*Laughs.*) Yes, I can see why conversation might be difficult.

GLUSHKO. You could be together again. A family! Xenia, we don't have time for this. Sergei's work today is too important...

XENIA. Have you asked Sergei if he wants a family?

GLUSHKO. Why wouldn't he want his family! Xenia...

XENIA. Comrade Glushko. Look at me. Do I look well? Do I look healthy?

GLUSHKO. What?

(*Floundering.*) Of course... you're a very... yes... you look well, you look wonderful! He'll be delighted to...

XENIA. *I* kept my job, Comrade Glushko. I kept my apartment. I'm still working in the same medical research department as I was when Sergei was arrested but, like you, I've been promoted.

GLUSHKO. Yes, but... what are you saying?

XENIA. That I understand why you can't talk freely with Sergei. It's difficult, isn't it? When you've betrayed him. Of course you had to. You had to live. You had to work. I understand... They keep you so long in the dark, don't they? Shouting, questions, questions, questions... Is Sergei Pavlovich a traitor? Is he a traitor, comrade? Tell us... It was so dark. Was it dark where they kept you?

I thought. Natasha wouldn't like the dark. I didn't know what might happen to Natasha. Children need sun to grow straight, don't they. They need it for healthy bones.

NATASHA (*quiet*). Mother, please don't...

GLUSHKO. You denounced him?

XENIA. Of course I did. I called him a traitor. And that word lies between us every time I see him, like a rotting fish. We can hardly bear to be in the same room with it. You didn't know? Well... why would he confide in you, of all people. I understand. Sergei doesn't talk freely with me either. No. I don't think we can be a family, Comrade Glushko.

GLUSHKO. Oh, but... surely... we'll give you the tour... we...

XENIA. No.

NATASHA. Mother, we can still visit him! I want to visit him. We can see him today. I'm glad we're here. I'm glad I'm seeing where he works.

Pause.

XENIA. Alright. Alright.

GLUSHKO. Would you like to freshen up? Come with me.

NATASHA, XENIA *and* GLUSHKO *move out of the way as* WORKERS *and* DESIGN ENGINEERS *are brought on by* GUARD TWO. *They take their places at work stations. The convention of the engineers' room is established. A level of intense concentration, of calculations, an impression of endless paperwork, hundreds of blueprints. A work space where all activity centres on one place – the place* KOROLYOV *will occupy.*

GUARD TWO. Alright! Get working!

The WORKERS/DESIGN ENGINEERS *start working, low-level activity. They're watching a central point, waiting for some other signal.*

KOROLYOV *is brought on by* GUARD TWO. *He takes his place at the centre of activity.*

KOROLYOV. Alright! Let's get working!

Instantly all the activity goes into hyperdrive. Everything is fed to KOROLYOV, *checked by him and passed out again.*

KOROLYOV *is completely absorbed in checking the figures. He throws the papers down.*

Which diseased piece of mule dung is responsible for this!

Everyone goes still, terrified. His deputy, MISHIN, *turns to the second designer,* IVANOVSKY.

MISHIN. I told you! I told you it wasn't ready!

IVANOVSKY *looks at the paperwork.*

IVANOVSKY. That would be my work.

KOROLYOV. You're a lying worm,

(*Indicating* MISHIN.) …it was this tub of rancid sausage.

MISHIN (*simultaneous*). Yes… but, SP, it wasn't my fault… we knew the deadline was…

IVANOVSKY (*simultaneous*). No, no, I take responsibility for the initial calculations…

KOROLYOV (*cutting over both of them*). You're both fired! Both of you! Get out of here!

MISHIN *and* IVANOVSKY *look at each other uncertainly then go back to the work stations.*

I said get out of here! Go on!

IVANOVSKY. But we can't, SP…

MISHIN. Come on, SP… it's a big day…

KOROLYOV. I know what day it is, Mishin! It's the day I finally kick your sorry, Stoli-soused arse out of my work-room. Get out!

IVANOVSKY. You know you can't fire us, no one can reassign a prisoner's labour except…

MISHIN (*to* IVANOVSKY, *warning*). Oleg!

IVANOVSKY (*under* MISHIN)….Comrade Glushko…

GLUSHKO *is approaching them.* KOROLYOV *sees him and beyond him, waiting,* XENIA *and* NATASHA.

KOROLYOV (*quiet*). Why's no one working?

(*Louder.*) Move, you drowsy excuses for engineers! Work!

The WORKERS/DESIGN ENGINEERS *get going again.*

GLUSHKO. Comrade Korolyov, is everything ready?

KOROLYOV. No.

GLUSHKO. What?

KOROLYOV. The figures are wrong. I told you we needed more time.

GLUSHKO. Then you'll have to… you'll have to…

Look, your family is here. You have to present this as a success, you have to tell them we've succeeded already!

KOROLYOV. I know what you want, Glushko.

XENIA. What does he want?

Pause.

GLUSHKO. I'll let you… I'll let you all… Natasha, talk to your father…

We don't have much time, Sergei!

GLUSHKO *moves off, anxiously checking the work.*

KOROLYOV. It's a big day for us. This is the day we have been told to present our completed work to the Politburo. Today is the triumphant conclusion to years of expensive labour.

XENIA (*picks up on his tone, looking round*). You're not ready.

KOROLYOV. A few weeks away.

XENIA. The design isn't working?

KOROLYOV. My part of the design is working.

XENIA (*gets it, indicating* GLUSHKO). Ah… so. The boss needs you to make him look good.

KOROLYOV. Yes.

How are you?

XENIA. As you see.

KOROLYOV. Natasha. Look at you.

NATASHA. I'm so glad, you've got windows.

KOROLYOV. What's that?

NATASHA. Every time I think of you working here I wonder if you can see the sun. And you can.

KOROLYOV. We've got windows. Rather dirty windows of course but...

NATASHA. I'm glad.

IVANOVSKY *sidles up, hesitant.*

IVANOVSKY. Excuse me... Comrade Koralyov...

He offers papers. KOROLYOV *looks at them.*

KOROLYOV. Well done, well done, good man.

(*To* XENIA.) Why did they bring you in here?

IVANOVSKY *moves away.*

XENIA. You want us to leave?

KOROLYOV. No! No of course not. How are you? How was the journey?

XENIA. Cold. The train was delayed longer than usual.

KOROLYOV. Have you eaten? Did you have enough food for the train?

MISHIN*'s turn to sidle up.*

MISHIN. Sergei, I'm so sorry...

KOROLYOV. It's alright, Vassily. Show me.

MISHIN (*offering papers*). I think we can suggest a probable solution to determining an accurate trajectory if...

KOROLYOV (*cutting him off; quiet*). Vassily, you think the bastards can count their own toes? It's fine. You've done well. We're ready for this.

MISHIN *moves away.*

(*To* XENIA). It's very good to see you.

I didn't expect to see you here.

XENIA. In the middle of your work. We're disturbing you.

KOROLYOV. No! It's... you look well, Xenia. You look... I'm glad to see you. Natasha, you look thin! Are you getting enough to eat?

XENIA. Comrade Glushko has offered us an apartment here.

KOROLYOV. Here?

XENIA. Yes. Here. In the middle of your work.

KOROLYOV. But how... why?

XENIA. So you see the advantages of making him look good.

KOROLYOV. You'd come here?

XENIA. You're asking us to come? That's what you want?

Pause.

KOROLYOV. What about Natasha's studies?

NATASHA. I'm finished this summer.

XENIA. Do you want us here?

KOROLYOV. Yes. Would you come?

XENIA. I don't know.

GLUSKO. It's nearly time. We need to be ready.

KOROLYOV. It's too sudden. We can... we'll have to talk about this later.

The GUARDS *rush the* WORKERS/DESIGN ENGINEERS *off apart from* MISHIN *and* IVANOVSKY.

XENIA. Glushko says you might be pardoned?

KOROLYOV. I've another ten years on my sentence. That hasn't changed.

XENIA. If they released you... if you were free, would you really come back to Moscow?

KOROLYOV. I don't understand you.

GLUSHKO. They're early! The cars! The cars are arriving!

XENIA. You didn't have to leave Moscow, Sergei.

KOROLYOV. I was asleep. We were *asleep*! How could I get away? They dragged me downstairs. They threw me in a van, Xenia!

XENIA. Sergei... you saw what was coming. All your colleagues were being arrested... all their families taken away...

KOROLYOV. So I should have denounced them first?

XENIA. Yes! For us! For our sake.

KOROLYOV. And our work? I should have just let it all be destroyed?

XENIA. Oh, your work!

NATASHA. Please. Please. Mother said you asked her to marry you over and over for six years.

XENIA. He did. He never stopped asking.

NATASHA. And at last you had to say yes.

XENIA. I had to say yes. He'd never have stopped asking. He never stops. Of course I said yes.

KOROLYOV. I was sure from the moment I saw you that I wanted to share my life with you. I'm still sure.

GLUSHKO. They have to go. Xenia, you have to go now.

WORKERS *and* DESIGN ENGINEERS *are clearing up, frantically getting ready.*

XENIA. I'm glad you asked me, Sergei. I'll always be glad you made me say yes. But you have to understand, I made my choice ten years ago. I won't move here. I won't leave my life. I can't bring Natasha to live under the shadow of a prison wall, with the smell of death and gunpowder in her nose. But your home is still your home, if you're free, if you want it.

GLUSHKO. If it all goes well, if we keep meeting our targets he'll be home with you soon.

XENIA. If his work can spare him.

GLUSHKO. Yes, yes, yes… we'll all be on holiday soon. I promise you both. I promise you, Sergei, if today goes well it'll be picnics by the Volga for all of us, now say goodbye.

XENIA. Goodbye.

KOROLYOV. Goodbye.

Goodbye, Natasha.

GLUSHKO. Goodbye, goodbye, goodbye! Go! Go!

He shoos them off. Turns to KOROLYOV.

Line up! Line up! Come on.

KOROLYOV, IVANOVSKY, MISHIN *and the other* WORKERS/DESIGN ENGINEERS *form a welcoming committee.*

Are we alright? Do I look alright?

IVANOVSKY *straightens* GLUSHKO*'s tie.*

Thank you. And Sergei, nothing about space today, you understand me? Not a word!

KHRUSHCHEV *and* BREZHNEV *enter, followed by members of the* POLITBURO.

GLUSHKO. Comrade First Secretary, honoured comrades… welcome… welcome. You'll take some tea? Vodka?

KHRUSHCHEV (*looking round*). Later, later, show us what we're paying for first.

GLUSHKO. Of course. Of course, as you can see our engineers have prepared for your visit. Everything is on schedule. We have exceeded Comrade Stalin's expectations…

KHRUSHCHEV. Comrade Stalin's dead.

GLUSHKO. Eh...

KHRUSHCHEV. Isn't he?

GLUSHKO. Yes.

KHRUSHCHEV. You noticed? You heard the news maybe?

GLUSHKO. Yes.

KHRUSHCHEV. So let's see if you can satisfy Comrade
Khrushchev's expectations. On you go.

GLUSHKO *is trying to hand out papers to* KHRUSHCHEV
and the others.

GLUSHKO. The eh... the initial work... the initial planning...
has proceeded as we anticipated...

KHRUSHCHEV. What work? What planning?

(*Re: the papers.*) These are pages of numbers! Why are you
showing me your numbers?

Is someone going to tell me what's going on here!?

KOROLYOV. Comrade Khrushchev, if I may...

KOROLYOV *leads them to the base of a rocket. They look up.*

A beat while they take it in.

KHRUSHCHEV. Why is it so big?

KOROLYOV. What you are looking at is our latest prototype
developed to carry liquid fuel. With this missile we hope to
increase our range by a factor of ten, allowing us to select
targets many thousands of miles away with reasonable
accuracy. As you know our deadline for completion was this
year...

KHRUSHCHEV. As you know? As you know? I don't know
anything. What is this thing?

KOROLYOV. It is an intercontinental ballistic missile.

KHRUSHCHEV. So what can it do?

KOROLYOV. This is our test model. We hope it can deliver a
warhead over a much longer distance than would previously
have been possible...

KHRUSHCHEV. How long?

KOROLYOV. It could reach America in just a few minutes.

KHRUSHCHEV. America? America?

KOROLYOV. Yes.

KHRUSHCHEV (*laughing, to the* POLITBURO). You hear that! You hear that? We've just made toy boats of their warships! Those guns of theirs are going to be good for nothing but salutes!

(*To* GLUSHKO.) Is it true!?

GLUSHKO. Yes, Comrade Khrushchev.

KHRUSHCHEV. Well, how many of these things do we have?

GLUSHKO. The Politburo, as you know, approved…

KHRUSHCHEV (*interrupts*). Look, you seem like a man who can understand plain talking, yes? I don't know what you were expecting today but this is how it is – the old bastard told me nothing. I don't know a fucking thing.

(*Pointing at the* MEMBERS OF THE POLITBURO.) They don't know a fucking thing.

Tell me again, slowly, so I can understand.

KOROLYOV. Comrade Stalin had a dream.

KHRUSHCHEV. Yes.

KOROLYOV (*as if quoting*). His dream was to plant missiles like saplings of a new forest, bent by the winds of the world to point wherever they were needed.

Their flight paths would be dotted lines of death threatening our enemies even in their own homes, as they threaten us now. He wanted to guard our whole, huge sky with fire and steel.

KHRUSHCHEV. He said that.

KOROLYOV. No. He had that written. But that was the idea.

KHRUSHCHEV. That was his dream.

KOROLYOV. Yes.

KHRUSHCHEV. Fucker never told me he had dreams.

Suddenly he bangs on the rocket.

(*To the* MEMBERS OF THE POLITBURO.) Look at this! Look at this thing, will you?!

(*To* KOROLYOV, *suddenly anxious*.) Oh, can I do that? It won't...?

KOROLYOV. It's quite safe.

KHRUSHCHEV *hits the rocket again.*

KHRUSHCHEV. That explains it, that explains the secret smile. You know the one I mean? Just peeking round the edges of his moustache with so much iron behind it. I thought death was the twinkle in the bastard's eye, the big punchline to every joke he ever told... But this is the big joke, isn't it? Ha!

KHRUSHCHEV *gives the rocket several more blows, laughing.*

He turns from examining the rocket to examining KOROLYOV.

Well. Well then.

What's your name?

KOROLYOV. Sergei Pavlovich Korolyov.

KHRUSHCHEV. And how are conditions in the missile-builders' prison. Sergei Pavlovich? Food alright is it? Plenty of fresh air?

KOROLYOV. Conditions are...

KHRUSHCHEV (*interrupts*). A fuck of a lot better than the Gulag. No, no, you're a lucky man, I can see that. And what was your sentence?

Pause.

KOROLYOV. Hard labour or death, Comrade Khrushchev.

KHRUSHCHEV. Comrade Stalin's rocket fuel. Got us all leaping forward, didn't it? Did you cry when he died?

KOROLYOV. I was... sad of course I...

KHRUSHCHEV. I wept like a child. He was our father. Now we're just children running from wolves...

He was right, of course he was right, the Americans are watching us from every wave of the sea. They're peering down on us from every patch of blue sky, ready to drop death on us whenever they like.

(*Suddenly to* MISHIN.) What did you do in the Great Patriotic War, comrade?

MISHIN. I...

I was in Czechoslovakia, Comrade First Secretary. I was a master of horses, in the cavalry...

KHRUSHCHEV. Wounded?

MISHIN. Yes, comrade.

KHRUSHCHEV. Show me.

Hesitant, MISHIN *pulls up his shirt to show his scar.*

Shrapnel.

MISHIN. The shell exploded right beside our position... I was the only one who survived...

KHRUSHCHEV (*stopping him*). It's alright, soldier. We've all got our wounds, eh?

We've given the world enough of our dead. We gave millions to win their war for them while they ate chocolate and chewed gum. The crops in our fields are still rich with the Russian blood that soaked into the earth – the blood of millions of farmers and soldiers who died winning that war. We broke the world's enemy for them and then the world turned round and threatened us?! Well, no more! No more! Ha! We'll show them! You'll show them, Sergei!

You've beaten the Americans and their pet Germans? They can't do this?

KOROLYOV. They're developing the German V2. But we don't think their design is yet capable of...

KHRUSHCHEV (*interrupts*). Oh, let me tell them! Let me tell them we can see a fly on a grain of wheat on their great plains and kill the fly and the whole plain with it…

KOROLYOV. Our accuracy is not yet…

KHRUSHCHEV. No! No, let me tell them that! I want to see their faces! Let them try and frighten our mothers and children now!

Do you have family, Sergei?

KOROLYOV. I've got a daughter.

KHRUSHCHEV. Wife and daughter, eh? Lovely. They let you see them?

Pause.

KOROLYOV. Yes, Comrade Khrushchev.

KHRUSHCHEV. Good, good, you'll spend days with them soon. Now your work's done.

KOROLYOV. The work is not completed.

GLUSHKO (*simultaneous*). Comrade Khrushchev…

KHRUSHCHEV (*simultaneous*). What!?

KOROLYOV. We do not have a working mathematical model, as yet. But if the work proceeds to our plan, the missile will fly within the month. I guarantee that.

KHRUSHCHEV. You guarantee that personally?

KOROLYOV. Yes, comrade.

KHRUSHCHEV. You know what I think then, Sergei Pavlovich? I think the people are going to pardon you. I think you'd still love Mother Russia even if you weren't staring down the barrel of a gun. Am I right?

KOROLYOV. You're right, comrade.

KHRUSHCHEV. So go and get your wife… You're a free man!

You can go out and buy your daughter a new pair of shoes. Have you got an apartment here for them?

GLUSHKO. Yes, Comrade Khrushchev…

KOROLYOV. No.

KHRUSHCHEV. What do you mean, 'No'?

KOROLYOV. They wouldn't come here.

They won't come, Comrade Khrushchev.

GLUSHKO. Comrade Khrushchev doesn't want to hear…

KHRUSHCHEV. She told you that?

KOROLYOV. Yes.

KHRUSHCHEV. Well… a man needs his family. Go to her.

GLUSHKO. We do need Sergei Pavlovich if the work is to proceed, Comrade Khrushchev…

KHRUSHCHEV. What about these other boys in white coats? They can finish the job without this lad here, can't they?

GLUSHKO. No.

KOROLYOV. No, Comrade Khrushchev.

GLUSHKO. Comrade Korolyov is indispensable. At the moment.

KHRUSHCHEV (*laughs*). And you're not?

Well.

Well, what are we going to do?

(*To* KOROLYOV.) All these plans, all these dreams of fire and steel in one little head? Is that wise? Is there room in there, comrade?

KOROLYOV. One mind can hold a million ideas, a million actions, as many possibilities as specks of light in the night sky.

KHRUSHCHEV. But put a bullet in his brain and you lose the lot. I can see how you managed to stay alive, comrade. Very clever.

Well, I'm still offering you a choice. You're pardoned. Take your freedom and go home to your wife if you like…

GLUSHKO (*cutting in*). Comrade Khrushchev…

KHRUSHCHEV. Shut up! I'm not talking to you!

(*To* KOROLYOV.) You decide, comrade. Do you need a holiday?

Pause.

KOROLYOV. No, comrade. I need to finish my work.

KHRUSHCHEV. Course you do.

KOROLYOV. I need Mishin, I need Ivanovsky. I need my team.

KHRUSHCHEV. Your team. Your team.

All enemies of the people?

No one answers.

Well… well, if a man has given his blood for the people I think that's all we need to know. I think that's all that counts in this new world, in these new days where our enemies want to bring us down while our wounds are still wet.

Let's try another way to fuel the rocket, comrades. The people will give you all their pardon. Do your work.

MISHIN *breaks down abruptly.*

KOROLYOV. Vassily…

KHRUSHCHEV. It's alright. Give him a drink.

(*To* MISHIN.) Take a drink, soldier.

Let's all have a drink.

The GUARDS *are handing round vodka.*

MISHIN *is still weeping.*

That's enough, that's enough now, we're celebrating now. You've done a good job, Sergei Pavlovich.

(*To* GLUSHKO.) He's done a good job for you, hasn't he? He's been a good deputy for your little rocket-building team.

(*To* KOROLYOV.) Who do you want as your deputy then?

(*Indicating* GLUSHKO.) Him?

KOROLYOV (*thrown*). Eh… I don't…

KHRUSHCHEV. You should be running this team, shouldn't you?

GLUSHKO. Comrade First Secretary…

KHRUSHCHEV (*cutting him off*). Shut up, we're not talking to you, Sergei and me are making a new plan now.

(*Indicating* GLUSHKO.) Do you need him?

Beat. KOROLYOV *looks at* GLUSHKO.

KOROLYOV. For what?

GLUSHKO. Everything we've done was dependant on my design for…

KHRUSHCHEV (*interrupts, just speaking to* KOROLYOV). So you can run your team and you have this one, unless you want him for your deputy?

GLUSHKO. No! No, the committee must approve any reorganisation in our working structure and…

KHRUSHCHEV (*turns on* GLUSHKO). Oh, must they? Which committee? Do I know them, have they bought me a drink recently, have any of them had their feet up on my chairs?

(*To* KOROLYOV.) You don't want him? You don't trust him?

When KOROLYOV *says nothing,* KHRUSHCHEV *indicates* BREZHNEV.

I trust this man to stand here, you see? Just behind me. He doesn't say much do you, Comrade Brezhnev?

BREZHNEV. No, comrade.

KHRUSHCHEV. He never has. He watches, and he sees it all, don't you?

BREZHNEV. Yes, comrade.

KHRUSHCHEV. And no one sees him. No one saw him until I did. I saw a boy who could learn what I had. I saw a young man who could follow me up the party. I saw a man who could take the trust I offered him and stand at my shoulder, my eyes and ears. Watching and listening until the blood and fire and bullets had passed us both by.

We understand each other, don't we? We understand what we must do now, for the people.

BREZHNEV. Yes, comrade.

KHRUSHCHEV. So, who do you want to stand beside you, Sergei?

Pause.

KOROLYOV. Vassily…

Comrade Mishin.

KHRUSHCHEV. The man who can stare down the barrel of a German tank! Yes! Good choice! More vodka, soldier!

GLUSHKO. Am I required here then?

KHRUSHCHEV. Those fucking Nazi shits! Every one of them sucking Uncle Sam's cock now, eh? But Sergei Pavlovich and the Soviet workers can beat them!

KOROLYOV. That's right, comrade, and we could beat them into space too.

GLUSHKO. Am I still required here!?

Pause.

KHRUSHCHEV. Are you drinking? No. Fuck off then.

Into space? What are you talking about? Take a drink, man.

GLUSHKO *exits.*

KOROLYOV. In a moment perhaps, Comrade Khrushchev, thank you. Can I show you something, Nikita Sergeyevich, can I show you my dream?

(*Drawing him over to the rocket again.*) Look, look, it's nearly touching the sky already. Over five million horsepower thrusting it up into the stars. Five tons of warhead soaring higher than any human thing ever made. We could escape gravity itself! We could send a satellite around the Earth!

KHRUSHCHEV. Why?

Why would we do that?

KOROLYOV. Because we must! It would be a first step, Comrade First Secretary. Before this, the idea of moving off the Earth, travelling beyond our little world has just been a dream. But we could make it real. Here, today, we could take that first step no one has dared to believe was possible. It would change what it means to be human.

No response.

Think of it, to take mankind so high, so high that we can look back and see what we are, look beyond the curve of the Earth to see what we can become!

No response.

For Mother Russia! For the love of our black earth and memory of our dead.

No response.

America will claim the first satellite very soon if we don't...

KHRUSHCHEV (*cuts him off*). You're ready to do this?

KOROLYOV. Almost immediately. We replace the warhead with a satellite, the plans have been submitted to the committee...

KHRUSHCHEV. Alright. Send everything to my office as well.

(*To* BREZHNEV.) You'll keep an eye on this?

BREZHNEV. Yes, comrade.

KHRUSHCHEV. You can have your dream, Sergei Pavlovich, as long as I have my missiles.

KHRUSHCHEV *and* BREZHNEV *exit. Once they are clear,* KOROLYOV, IVANOVSKY, MISHIN *and the others roar with delight, dancing and hugging each other.*

MISHIN. A toast! A toast! To the new chief designer! More vodka!

The GUARD *is holding the vodka bottle.* KOROLYOV *goes to face him.*

KOROLYOV. I think we can take charge of that now. Don't you?

GUARD TWO. Of course, Comrade Chief Designer. Excuse me…

KOROLYOV (*taking the bottle*). You're excused. You're all excused. No more work today.

The GUARDS exits followed by WORKERS and DESIGN ENGINEERS whooping, carrying vodka. MISHIN, IVANOVSKY and KOROLYOV remain.

MISHIN (*snatching the bottle off KOROLYOV*). To the chief designer!

Filling everyone's glasses.

Come on, SP, one drink.

KOROLYOV *lets him fill the glass but doesn't drink.*

KOROLYOV (*to IVANOVSKY*). How come this wet baboon cries with joy at the thought of working with me and you don't even blink?

IVANOVSKY. I've no tears left in me, SP, you know that.

KOROLYOV. Oh, I'll find your tears. The way I'll work you now…

Bring her out. Let's look at her.

From a hiding place, IVANOVSKY produces a scale model of Sputnik. A beautiful shining silver ball.

He holds it up.

We're going to make you real, beautiful. We're going to let you grow and fire you up where you belong.

They're passing the Sputnik among them. MISHIN kisses it.

MISHIN. You little darling.

KOROLYOV. Hey! Hey! No marks!

He polishes the model with his sleeve.

We're going to polish the skin till it blazes with all the light of the sun, so we can see her pass over us with our own eyes, the star we made.

IVANOVSKY. I have to tell the others, can I tell them, Sergei?

KOROLYOV. Yes! Go on! Take a bottle.

IVANOVSKY runs off.

MISHIN. That was your daughter?

KOROLYOV. Yes. That was Natasha.

MISHIN. She's lovely. A lovely girl.

KOROLYOV. Yes.

MISHIN. Take a drink, Sergei.

MISHIN exits.

KOROLYOV picks up his glass.

The OLD MAN *appears from the shadows around the rocket.*

OLD MAN. A rocket?

A rocket is no memorial, is it, Sergei? Sergei Pavlovich, you know full well all I wanted was another sugar lump.

Dip it in vodka, melt it on your tongue, then drain the rest and think of me.

KOROLYOV *hesitates, looking at the glass, then he pours it out.*

What a fucking waste.

KOROLYOV *raises his little shining Sputnik.*

KOROLYOV. You're lovely. A lovely thing.

Fly up and see who chases you. If the race starts we'll all run to the other side of the Moon.

KOROLYOV *throws the Sputnik up into the sky.*

Lights down.

The silver sound of Sputnik overhead.

A parade ground, Central Russia, An autumn night. October 4th 1957.

SOLDIERS *from the local barracks and* YOUNG WOMEN *from a textile factory dancing together.* YURI *is dancing*

with VALYA. KOMAROV, TITOV *and* LEONOV *are
dancing with other* WOMEN *or, in the absence of partners,
boisterously with each other. The dance finishes, an*
OFFICER *shouts over the end.*

OFFICER. Last dance! One more then flying officers report
back to barracks!

The music begins again, they dance.

YURI *is talking to* VALYA.

YURI. So I'll see you next week then.

VALYA *laughs.*

What?

VALYA. Every time!

Have you asked me if I want to see you next week?

YURI. No.

VALYA. Are you going to?

YURI. No.

VALYA. Why not?

YURI. Because I know the answer.

VALYA. You're very sure of yourself.

YURI. No, I'm sure of you.

VALYA. You...!

Words fail her, she starts to pull away.

YURI (*stopping her*). No, you don't get it.

If I asked if you wanted to see me next week you'd say you
didn't know, wouldn't you?

VALYA *hesitates.*

But I know. I'm sure.

VALYA. Of what?

YURI. That I want to see you.

VALYA. And that's enough, is it?

YURI. Isn't it? You don't trust me?

VALYA. Why should I trust you?

YURI. Look at me. I'm so sure I want you, Valya. Look, can't you see it in my eyes?

VALYA. Let me see your hands.

He offers them. She looks at them.

My mother taught me how to read a man's hands.

(*Studying them.*) If there's dirt under the nails the man will bring his working day home to make your nights a misery.

YURI. I'm clean.

VALYA. If the nails are clean but there are cracks in his skin, his working day will break him in the end.

YURI. Clean and smooth.

VALYA. And those are the hands of a thief who lives off the work of others…

(*Seeing something.*) What is this? On your skin?

YURI. What are you seeing?

VALYA. It's silver.

YURI. Oh, it's from the engines, little flakes of metal.

VALYA. You clean the engines of the planes?

YURI. No, no, I stroke them, before I fly. Like horses.

VALYA. Horses?

YURI. A jet engine's a tricky thing. You don't know how it might decide to kill you. A wild horse is an easier beast to tame than a MiG landing on a frozen runway. So I always pat the engines before I throw my life into the sky. I ask them to be sweet one more time. It can't hurt, can it? I'm still here, aren't I?

OFFICER. That's it, Lieutenant! Time's up!

VALYA. You have to go.

YURI. No. We've got a moment.

VALYA. It's cold. Can you smell it, in the air? Snow. Smells like smoke and sugar. There'll be no more dancing on the parade ground after tonight. Just you squaddies stamping up and down, kicking the ice off your boots.

YURI. Flying officers don't stamp, we walk on air.

So I'll see you next week.

VALYA. I don't know. I don't know how to be sure.

YURI. What did your mother say about men with metal hands?

VALYA. She doesn't know any.

YURI. Need to make up your own mind then.

LEONOV runs on, waving a radio over his head. He's shouting over the music.

LEONOV. Sputnik! Sputnik! Sputnik!

The music dies away as LEONOV reaches YURI.

Yuri, it's Sputnik!

(*Shouting the noise down.*) Listen! Listen!

Silence. The silvery sound of Sputnik, faint through the radio, growing louder.

VALYA. What is it?

LEONOV. The world's first satellite!

TITOV. My God, it's up there now. It's above us!

KOMAROV. Can you see it?

TITOV. It's too small. It won't be visible to the naked eye.

LEONOV. There! Look! Shining!

VALYA. It's a star, a moving star.

KOMAROV (*pointing*). No it's there!

VALYA. I'm seeing it everywhere. The whole sky's full of moving stars.

TITOV. It's snow. It's snowing.

Snow starts to fall on their upturned faces.

OFFICER. Fall in, men, fall in, it's time.

KOMOROV. Everyone else is lined up.

LEONOV. Yuri, we have to go.

The others move off, still looking up till only YURI *and* VALYA *are left.*

YURI. They'll hear it over all of Russia. Over the whole world. The sky is ours.

VALYA. Is it really true?

YURI. I'll bring you a piece of sky, a star to hang round your neck. I'll pick it next time I fly up there.

VALYA. Listen to you. Next you'll tell me that's stardust on your hands.

YURI. No. It's just oil and metal.

(*Takes her hands.*) But the thing about metal…

The thing about metal is, you make it one shape and that's how it'll be. It's true. The only thing that wears metal out is time and it'll last a whole life before that happens.

So what do you want, Valya Goryacheva?

VALYA *kisses him.*

OFFICER. Lieutenant Gagarin!

YURI. Coming, sir!

YURI exits. VALYA exits slowly in the opposite direction, still looking up at the sky.

The following scenes flow into this one, characters from one entering as the previous actor is still exiting.

A park, Moscow, continuous.

The snow is falling a little quicker. NATASHA walks through the park, across the stage, a radio in her hands, listening to the sound of Sputnik, watching the sky.

The Gulag, Kolyma, continuous.

As NATASHA *exits, a* GULAG PRISONER *crawls onstage, breath rasping. The snow is falling fast and fierce now. The* DOCTOR *enters, wrapped up against the weather. She has a radio too, the sound of Sputnik is replaced by a patriotic commentary explaining the triumph of Sputnik, it's in Russian, the commentator rousing and excited, the signal is fading in and out. The* DOCTOR *is trying to get another channel, banging the radio and muttering. She doesn't see the* GULAG PRISONER *at first.*

DOCTOR. Come on! Come on! Some music, not this shit! I want music, fuck, I'll settle for a military band, come on!

She sees the GULAG PRISONER.

Where are you going?

Where are you going, come back to the infirmary, you'll die out here.

GULAG PRISONER. Leave me alone…

I want to die… in the clean air… I don't want… your medicine… poison…

DOCTOR. I don't have any medicine. I just count the dead. Come on, don't die yet. Come inside.

She pulls at him.

GULAG PRISONER. Bitch.

DOCTOR. Yeah, yeah…

She tries to heave him up. He cries out in pain.

Come on. Come on, you bastard! Fight, damn you…!

She can't lift him.

GULAG PRISONER. I want… to die… under… the open sky…

She lets him drop.

DOCTOR. I'm so sorry. I'm sorry. Why should you stay alive to make me feel better? What's your name? What's your name?

The GULAG PRISONER *mumbles something indistinct.*

That's your prison number. What's your name?

Never mind. Never mind. Think about... something happy... something warm. Did you love your mother?

GULAG PRISONER. Mum...

DOCTOR. Yes. Can you see her? Where is she?

GULAG PRISONER. My mother... My mother sat me on... a red rug... in the window... she pulled me close...

DOCTOR. That's right. That's right and nothing's going to hurt any more...

GULAG PRISONER. I could see... the reflections of the candle flames in the glass. I could see... the candles above in the dark... a thousand candles... stars in the sky...

She's got the dose ready to inject him.

DOCTOR. It's alright. It'll be warm, it'll be quiet and I'll hold you till you get there.

GULAG PRISONER. She said... she said... you can't touch the stars, Pavel... they're too far away... you'll have to travel miles through the dark to reach them.

DOCTOR (*rolling up his sleeve*). Shhhh...

GULAG PRISONER. And I said... then I will...

The DOCTOR *injects him. The* GULAG WORKER *stiffens then goes still.*

The patriotic voice on the radio rises to a crescendo.

RADIO. Sputnik! Sputnik!

The silvery sound of Sputnik.

The DOCTOR *looks up into the falling snow.*

DOCTOR. Sputnik.

She spits.

End of Act One.

ACT TWO

Scene One

The DESIGN ENGINEERS' *room.*

MISHIN, IVANOVSKY *and* KOROLYOV *are watching a piece of soundless film.*

We don't see the film itself.

MISHIN. Where is this?

IVANOVSKY. America.

MISHIN. Yes but where?

IVANOVSKY. Oh, like you'd know.

KOROLYOV. Florida.

MISHIN. Florida? Are you sure? It looks very dry.

KOROLYOV. This is their most recent unmanned prototype. It's still basically the V2, don't you think?

·IVANOVSKY. I don't know.

MISHIN. Do they farm there? It looks too dry. They have a lot of cattle, don't they... the Americans. I think that land's too dry for cattle.

IVANOVSKY. I'd say they've changed the fuel.

KOROLYOV. That's what the intelligence says, but...

MISHIN. Maybe a different kind of cow. Do you think that's it?

IVANOVSKY. I don't understand why they've changed the shape.

MISHIN. They've only put two engines on the thing, so they must have about 120,000 kilo thrust, kerosene oxygen fuel maybe?

KOROLYOV. This is why he's second in command.

IVANOVSKY. Oh, is that why?

MISHIN. Enough to get them into orbit.

KOROLYOV. Maybe. Let's see.

IVANOVSKY. Here she goes.

KOROLYOV. That is an elegant shape, look at that white slender nose...

MISHIN. She's wobbling.

IVANOVSKY. No, she's going up.

KOROLYOV. Beautiful aristocratic American nose, sniffing out the Moon...

MISHIN. Sergei, you already know if they launched successfully, just tell us.

IVANOVSKY. She's still going up, steady as a piston...

MISHIN. I think there's a tremor... there... no?

IVANOVSKY. No... Maybe... Oooh!

They all groan in horror and delight.

MISHIN. Did you see that!

IVANOVSKY. Boom! Look at her burn!

MISHIN. They can't do it!

IVANOVSKY. Boom!

MISHIN. Forget it, forget it, America, spend your money on new cars. You haven't got the rocket engineers to match Oleg and Vassily!

KOROLYOV. It's old film.

MISHIN. We've beaten them!

KOROLYOV. Intelligence kept it for months. It's old.

IVANOVSKY. But we've beaten them.

KOROLYOV. They're bound to have made some progress since then...

MISHIN. But...!!??

KOROLYOV. But right now... *we've beaten them!*

America is lying in the dirt staring up at our vapour trail!
The first man in space is going to be a good Soviet citizen,
no question.

IVANOVSKY. Yes!

KOROLYOV. Alright. Run it again. Let's work out what they
might have done next.

GENERAL GELADZE *enters. He salutes.*

GELADZE. The cosmonauts are ready for your inspection,
Comrade Chief Designer.

KOROLYOV. Yes, yes...

In a minute.

GELADZE. All good boys. Trained and ready...

KOROLYOV, MISHIN *and* IVANOVSKY *are ignoring
him, absorbed in the film again.*

KOROLYOV. There is something about that nose. Why make it
like that?

GELADZE. One metre seventy-eight tall, as requested, all
trained, you'll see...

Though we're all puzzling about that one. One metre
seventy...

IVANOVSKY. It's just vanity. There's no reason. There can't be
an aerodynamic benefit at that thrust.

GELADZE. As Uncle Joe would say, 'Do the work, comrade,
and ask the party for the reason...'

They all look at him.

KOROLYOV. What?

GELADZE. Our Uncle Joe Stalin would have got the reason out
of you, eh?

KOROLYOV. What are you talking about?

GELADZE. Why are all the cosmonauts to be under one metre seventy-eight?

And seventy-five kilos?

KOROLYOV. To fit in the capsule.

GELADZE. Of course. Of course.

(*Laughing.*) Stupid of me.

They ignore him again.

MISHIN (*re: the film*). You see the tremor starts as soon as it's cleared the gantry…

GELADZE. Well, you've got a good bunch. They're the right height and they're ready to die.

KOROLYOV. That won't be required.

GELADZE. If it is they're ready. They are heroes. Heroes of the Soviet people.

KOROLYOV. Good.

I'll be with you in a moment.

GELADZE. Of course. 'Scuse me, 'scuse me, comrades, getting in your way. You're busy men. Excuse me.

I'll wait for you outside, Comrade Chief Designer.

GELADZE *exits.*

KOROLYOV. I better get this over with. Tell me what you think when I get back later. Work it out for me.

MISHIN. Heroes of the Soviet people, eh? Is that what you ordered, Sergei?

KOROLYOV. Of course.

MISHIN. Of course you did. Just what we need. More of those.

IVANOVSKY *shushes him, laughing but shocked. They exit.*

The COSMONAUTS' *training room.*

The COSMONAUTS, LEONOV, KOMAROV, TITOV *and* YURI, *are standing, waiting, rigidly at attention.*

After a few motionless moments, YURI *looks at his fellow* COSMONAUTS. *He looks round.*

There's something really hot and metal right beside them. A heating pipe, a piece of equipment, a samovar. YURI *reaches out and touches it briefly, looking at the others. He winces in pain at the heat, blowing on his fingers. He touches it again, checking he's got everyone's attention. Snatches his hand off again.*

YURI. Five roubles says I last two minutes.

He waits, hand poised expectantly. An uncertain moment then all the COSMONAUTS *break ranks, slapping one hand on the same bit of metal. They hold the hot metal, wincing and gasping in discomfort.*

LEONOV *breaks first, dancing away, waving his heated fingers.*

KOMAROV *follows seconds later.* YURI *and* TITOV *are still holding it.*

LEONOV. Go on, Yuri!

KOMAROV. Gherman's steady.

LEONOV. Go on, Yuri!

KOMAROV. Ten roubles on Gherman.

LEONOV. You've got him! You've got him! You...

YURI *lets go.*

Shit, comrade, what happened?

YURI. Yeah, like you were still in there.

Nice one, Titov.

TITOV *is still holding on.*

LEONOV. Titov?

KOMAROV. Gherman, you've won.

YURI. Look at him!

KOMAROV. Gherman, drop it.

YURI. He's going purple, look.

LEONOV. You've won!

KOMAROV. You've won!

YURI. You beat me, man, come on!

TITOV *drops it.*

TITOV. 'Upon the brink of the wild stream
He stood, and dreamt a mighty dream.'

LEONOV. Who did?

TITOV. Pushkin.

KOMAROV. It's a quote.

LEONOV. Right.

YURI *slaps out his damaged hand.*

YURI. Well done!

TITOV *returns the shake with force.*

Ow! Ow!

(*Laughing.*) Alright, you got me again.

TITOV *lets him go.*

Can you still bend your fingers? Shit, that was stupid, they
might have us trying out the instrument panel.

TITOV. I used my left hand.

YURI (*to others*). See?

He wins again. Can't get past you, can we, Titov?

TITOV. You can try if you like.

YURI *tries to step past* TITOV, TITOV *blocks him. They
move, block, move, block – faster and faster till they are
actually wrestling each other.*

GELADZE *enters with* KOROLYOV.

GELADZE. Cosmonauts!

They quickly get back in line, standing to attention.

KOROLYOV. So, here you all are. My little eagles.

Relax. Come on, I'm just going to explain things to you.

GELADZE. At ease.

The COSMONAUTS *relax.*

KOROLYOV. This is how it works, boys. We're building you a craft to take you out of the Earth's atmosphere.

You're all top pilots but all you have to do is monitor its performance.

As you know we've tested the rocket with dogs. The dogs that orbited and landed again all lived. Some of them did not land.

The DOCTOR *enters and stands, watching and listening.*

But if I've done my job this one will. Don't worry, boys. I'm good at my job.

So we've tested our design. You'll get a chance to sit in the capsule in a moment.

YURI *starts to take off his shoes.*

You'll see it is a simple practical structure. I can show you the blueprints so you understand everything. We design the parts. We send the designs to the factory. They send us back the parts. We fit them together. Simple. Like building a tractor or one of your MiGs we...

Sees YURI.

What are you doing, comrade?

GELADZE. Lieutenant Gagarin, get up, what are you doing?

YURI. You said we were going to get in the capsule, comrade. So I thought...

KOROLYOV. What?

YURI. Well... we've got to take our shoes off, comrade... it's only polite...

GELADZE. You brainless excuse for a flying officer, Gagarin! What do you think you're going to do, fly the designer's machine in your socks?

KOROLYOV. He's thinking about keeping the farm dirt off the floor.

(*To* YURI.) Is that it?

You'd take your shoes off before you went in your uncle's house, wouldn't you, Gagarin?

YURI. Of course.

KOROLYOV. Good for you, farm boy.

The other COSMONAUTS *look at each other then drop and start pulling off their boots.* KOROLYOV *talks to* YURI *over this.*

Where are you from?

YURI. Smolensk.

KOROLYOV. A farmer's boy from Smolensk. Of course. I've heard they're all thieves in Smolensk, what do you say?

YURI. It's a hard life farming that earth. If you're not born into luck maybe you need to steal some.

KOROLYOV. So you're all thieves?

YURI. We're all lucky.

KOROLYOV. And how far do you think your luck will get you here? You'll have to learn something here, Lieutenant.

(*To all of them.*) We can't tell you everything in one day. We're going to prepare classes so you can learn the system thoroughly. You'll attend lectures and then we'll set you some exams.

YURI *has raised his hand.*

Yes?

YURI. Will you be marking us, Comrade Chief Designer?

KOROLYOV. Yes and I'll throw you out! Stop smiling! What are you smiling at, you featherless sparrow!?

He waits, face close to YURI. YURI *keeps his eyes front. Face blank.*

Alright.

Alright, go through, little eagles. My boys and girls will get you ready.

The COSMONAUTS *exit carrying their boots.*

One of those boys is going to see beyond the edges of the world.

GELADZE. Lieutenant Gagarin is the perfect proletarian candidate.

KOROLYOV. Is he?

GELADZE. A tractor driver's son…

(*Showing* KOROLYOV.) You see I've kept extensive notes on all the cosmonauts… see here, Gagarin… honourable proletarian background… good performance in all tests… you see? Here and… here…

KOROLYOV. He's good but he's not the best, is he?

GELADZE. Well, in a sense, comrade, he is the best because he…

KOROLYOV (*interrupts, pointing*). Here… and here… and here… Titov… first… best performance, first, first, best, best…

Beat.

GELADZE. Titov. Of course. Of course. An able candidate. But Gagarin is my recommendation.

KOROLYOV. Well… I'll consider your recommendation.

GELADZE. I am responsible for the military personnel, comrade. As Uncle Joe would say, each man has only one part to play in the revolution so play it well.

KOROLYOV *starts to leave.*

If I could make another suggestion, comrade?

KOROLYOV. Yes?

GELADZE. Your team… at their current rate of progress the launch will be delayed.

KOROLYOV. It might.

GELADZE. Then they should sleep less.

KOROLYOV. What?

GELADZE. Men can work quite efficiently with six hours' sleep in every forty-eight. That's been proven in combat.

KOROLYOV. Has it?

GELADZE. I've witnessed it myself.

KOROLYOV. Well. Thank you for sharing your valuable experience, comrade. However, I'm responsible for the timetable my team work to, or I was last time I checked.

GELADZE. Of course, of course, comrade, stupid of me...

What are the chances of success, Comrade Chief Designer?

Pause.

KOROLYOV. Fifty-fifty.

GELADZE. That's good. Yes.

KOROLYOV. Good enough to try? Yes. I hope so.

KOROLYOV *is exiting. He sees the* DOCTOR. *He stops dead, staring at her.*

DOCTOR. Shall I set up the next tests, General?

GELADZE. Yes. They'll be back with you shortly.

KOROLYOV *is still staring at the* DOCTOR.

Comrade Chief Designer?

KOROLYOV *and* GELADZE *exit.*

Scene Two

The COSMONAUTS' *training room.*

The DOCTOR *and* TECHNICIANS *are using medical-testing equipment.*

All the COSMONAUTS *enter and start to work, running on a treadmill, whirling in a wire centrifuge, swinging upside down.*

They get faster and faster...

The DOCTOR *is timing them, taking readings.*

DOCTOR. Stop!

They stop, exhausted.

Change.

Quickly they change positions and start again. Faster and faster.

Stop!

They're completely wiped out. A TECHNICIAN *brings on the* GUINEA PIG *in a wheelchair. The* GUINEA PIG *is parked to the side as the* TECHNICIAN *waits for the* COSMONAUTS.

Lieutenants Titov and Leonov, they're ready for you in the oxygen tank... Lieutenants Komorov and Gagarin, take your clothes off, please.

YURI. Why? What are we doing now?

DOCTOR. Just take your clothes off please, Lieutenant.

TITOV. We're doing the oxygen-deprivation test again?

TECHNICIAN. They're ready for you, Lieutenant Titov. They're waiting.

TITOV. We've done the oxygen-deprivation test three times today. He passed out in three minutes. I passed out in three and a half. Every time. What do you think will happen this time?

LEONOV. Gherman, it's fine...

TITOV. We haven't slept for four days. Alright. We're used to that. We haven't eaten for four days. Alright. We can take that.

But what is the point of repeating and repeating and repeating that oxygen-deprivation test? If the capsule loses integrity we're dead! If our oxygen system fails we're dead! Do we need to rehearse it?

The DOCTOR *turns to the* GUINEA PIG.

DOCTOR. Comrade. Tell the Lieutenant your record in the oxygen-deprivation tank.

GUINEA PIG. Four minutes.

The DOCTOR *is showing* TITOV *papers.*

DOCTOR. I recorded it. See?

TITOV. Who is he?

DOCTOR. He's the tester, Lieutenant Titov. He finds the limit and then we push you to it.

TITOV. He's been in the oxygen-deprivation tank for four minutes?

GUINEA PIG. And ten seconds.

DOCTOR. Long enough to effect a re-entry I'm told. If you can stay awake to do it, cosmonaut?

TITOV *exits, followed by* LEONOV *and the* TECHNICIAN.

Your clothes, Lieutenant?

YURI *starts to undress. His attention is on the* GUINEA PIG.

YURI. I've seen you, haven't I?

GUINEA PIG. I was in the hot room. Just before they sent you in, Comrade Gagarin.

YURI. I thought that was you! Are you alright now?

GUINEA PIG. I'm fine now. They cooked me though, comrade. Till the hairs on my arms were smoking. Till the tears in my eyes baked away. Till I could smell my own shit roasting... more than that maybe but I don't remember, I passed out... look...

He shows YURI *a scar on his head.*

That's where I hit my head on the metal bench going down. I've frozen for you too.

YURI. For me?

The DOCTOR *is checking* YURI's *heart, etc.*

DOCTOR. The testers find the limit. And then we push you to it.

GUINEA PIG. That's my job, freezing and burning and losing
every meal I ever swallow for the sake of the little eagles.
Today, right... oh, today was a killer, they put us in the
centrifuge, at full speed, spun us till our eyeballs scrambled,
till our blood's foaming like gassy beer...

Seven minutes I was in there...

YURI. Seven. No, they never take us past two.

DOCTOR. Lieutenant Komorov, you are dismissed for today.
Lieutenant Gagarin, please.

GUINEA PIG. No, they don't take you past two, comrade,
because a few of us got broken up after three minutes or so,
but I lasted... It's only ten gs. I'm still here.

You know the catapult sled?

YURI. No.

GUINEA PIG. You will, comrade, you will! It's to test what
impact you could survive. They strap us in and fire us at the
wall... Bam! I've seen more stars than you ever will, Comrade
Gagarin, however far they send you... that sled takes you up
to forty gs for a microsecond. But that's alright. I'm alive.

I find the limit so you can follow without hurting yourself.
Like a sniffer dog in a minefield.

The GUINEA PIG *is coughing, clearly not right, keeping it
upbeat but fighting pain.*

YURI. Do you want to sort him out?

DOCTOR. Just a moment...

GUINEA PIG. Yeah... well, they said to us when we
volunteered, we've tried this stuff on dogs and only fifty per
cent of them died... well, a man's stronger than a dog, isn't
he?

The GUINEA PIG *cries out in pain.* YURI *pulls away from
the* DOCTOR *and goes to him.*

YURI. Come and sort him out!

The DOCTOR *hesitates then, impatient, starts preparing
pain relief.*

GUINEA PIG. You're a great pilot, Comrade Gagarin. I wanted to be a pilot but... you know... there's the written exam too...

YURI. Yeah, that's a killer.

Forget being a pilot. You're a hero, man, that's what you are.

GUINEA PIG. Never going to fly the rocket but...

YURI. Oh right, you'll never get to lie back in a comfy chair and get a free joyride... no you won't, will you? They've got better things for the hard men to do than sit in armchairs. Fuck me, I'm really depressed now. You find the limit and I can't even get close enough behind you to see it.

Have they got you somewhere decent to live around here?

GUINEA PIG. Comrade Gagarin, you won't believe it. Our own apartment. Our own bathroom.

YURI. In the new blocks? Just south of the airfield?

GUINEA PIG. Beautiful.

YURI. They put us in there. The stairs still smell sweet! The stairwells smell of new paint!

GUINEA PIG. And warm! Every apartment warm and heated. It's a new world, comrade. We're getting the new world they promised us. Even my mother...

YURI. Yeah?

GUINEA PIG. She's out at Rynok, near Stalingrad? She wrote to me. 'Nikolai, I have warm feet.' The first winter of her life she's had warm boots. No holes! No stitches splitting from the soles! New boots. Her own brand-new winter boots.

The DOCTOR *injects him.*

YURI. It's a new world. My wife... Valya...

GUINEA PIG. Yes?

YURI. Last time I was home she'd bought ice cream.

GUINEA PIG. Yes?

KOROLYOV *enters under this.*

YURI. To celebrate. There's a man, just at the end of our street, you'll have to look for him, he's selling ice cream. Anyone can buy it, kids, old people, ice cream all day. She bought everything he had left she was so happy.

GUINEA PIG. Oh, I want a taste of that.

YURI. 'We're going to celebrate, Yuri,' she says, 'I went to work on the maternity ward at the hospital today and every baby was clean and every baby was fat and every baby was alive.'

GUINEA PIG. A new world.

YURI. And you're one of the heroes making it, comrade. You're showing us. Nothing we can't do.

GUINEA PIG (*drifting out of consciousness*). Need to make… a fat baby… of your own, cosmonaut.

YURI. Working on it, comrade.

The GUINEA PIG *is unconscious.* YURI *looks round, sees* KOROLYOV.

Comrade Chief Designer.

KOROLYOV. It's alright, Lieutenant. At ease.

YURI (*to* DOCTOR). Will he be alright?

DOCTOR. I expect so.

It's fifty-fifty.

What do you think of those odds?

YURI. I've beaten worse.

DOCTOR. I bet you have.

The TECHNICIANS *enter with a trolley. They lift the* GUINEA PIG *onto it.*

(*To* TECHNICIANS.) I'll check he's stable then you can come back and get him. Escort Lieutenant Gagarin back to quarters.

YURI. I'll stay with him. Till he comes round.

DOCTOR. No. Those wards are restricted. Run along.

YURI. I can help him down there.

DOCTOR. You've got a great smile, Lieutenant, but it won't get you everything you want.

YURI. Fifty per cent?

KOROLYOV. He can check back on him before you take him down.

The DOCTOR *gives him a look, then she nods.*

YURI *and the* TECHNICIANS *exit.*

KOROLYOV. I know you… don't I?

DOCTOR. Do you?

KOROLYOV. Yes. Yes.

It's you.

DOCTOR. Is it?

KOROLYOV. Yes.

DOCTOR. I doubt it. I doubt I'm who you think I am.

KOROLYOV. No. No it is you! I'm certain.

DOCTOR. If you say so.

The DOCTOR *is working on the* GUINEA PIG. *Hooking up a drip or otherwise readying him to be moved.*

You look well, Sergei Pavlovich.

KOROLYOV. I am well.

DOCTOR. You look happy.

KOROLYOV. I am happy. You on the other hand look as miserable as a toothless cat in a bucket of fish.

DOCTOR. I did twenty years in the Gulag, Sergei, long years, war years, you only had to suffer five. No. I don't think I'm who you think I am any more.

KOROLYOV. I'll do what I can.

DOCTOR. Who for?

KOROLYOV. For you.

DOCTOR (*to unconscious* GUINEA PIG). Oh, bad luck,
comrade, the chief designer can't get you that hero's medal.

I was promised an apartment.

KOROLYOV. Alright... Alright, I'll look into it.

DOCTOR. Three rooms.

KOROLYOV. No one gets three rooms.

DOCTOR. Not even if they've saved the life of the chief
designer?

KOROLYOV. And how many did you kill?

DOCTOR. Don't you talk to me about death. Don't you dare
talk to me about death, Sergei Pavlovich!

I have an army whispering at my back and they're all saying
the same thing. 'Why is he breathing when we're not? Why
is he sucking our air into his lungs? Who is he? Who is he?'

The OLD MAN *enters under this, crosses the action.*

KOROLYOV. I'm your boss and you'll be reassigned.

DOCTOR. I answer to the medical team. They answer to
General Geladze. What's the matter, Sergei? You worried I'll
kill one of your precious eagle chicks before you do?

Have you decided who you're sending up first?

KOROLYOV *doesn't answer.*

DOCTOR. Well, they're in great condition. They're all superb
pilots. They all have regular bowel movements and great
shoulders. Flip a coin.

KOROLYOV. I'm not sending anyone up there to get killed.

OLD MAN. This isn't the time. I'm feeling lucky.

DOCTOR. Can you be certain they won't?

OLD MAN. I could steal my own soul back from death if I put
my mind to it. But they tell me good men have no souls these
days.

The OLD MAN *starts to exit.*

DOCTOR. Life and death, Comrade Chief Designer. How does it feel? How will you choose?

KOROLYOV. I'll send a lucky man.

Scene Three

Bunker, the Voshtok launch pad.

YURI *is high above the bunker, he's facing the sky.*

KOROLYOV, IVANOVSKY *and* TECHNICIANS *are working below.*

KOROLYOV *can speak to* YURI *through a microphone.*

KOROLYOV. Before I pull your head off your shoulders, Oleg, and tie a knot in your *neck*!... Tell me what the delay is this time?

IVANOVSKY. Birds, on the gantry.

KOROLYOV. Shoot them!

MISHIN *enters, speaking quietly to* KOROLYOV.

MISHIN. I have the letters.

KOROLYOV. What letters?

MISHIN. Our statements. To the people? You told me to prepare our statements for broadcast so...

KOROLYOV. Yes, yes, let me see.

MISHIN *shows him three letters, one after the other.*

MISHIN. If he lands on enemy territory...

KOROLYOV (*pushing it back at him*). If he lands on enemy territory we won't be saying anything to the people, will we? This one?

MISHIN. Announcing our successful orbit. The first man in space.

KOROLYOV (*reading*). Good. Good.

Holds out his hand for the next.

MISHIN (*handing it over*). If he dies.

KOROLYOV (*reads, hands it back, instructs* MISHIN).
Beloved son of the Soviet people.

MISHIN. You said keep the tone official so…

KOROLYOV. Beloved son. He's a beloved son! Change it.

TITOV enters, suited up.

Two hours! Two hours he's been up there while you brainless
dung beetles try to remember how to think!

(*Into microphone, completely different tone.*) You bored,
Yuri? Did they get you some music yet?

(*Screaming at crew again.*) I told you to get him some music.
Where are the records! Put a song on for the man!

KOROLYOV *is hunting around for records.*

YURI. No, no, comrade, it's fine. I've got a… I think they're
playing me a love song.

KOROLYOV. So they should.

Above them YURI starts to sing quietly.

TITOV (*to* IVANOVSKY). I can stand down?

IVANOVSKY (*working*). Once the hatch is sealed, Comrade
Lieuetenant.

TITOV. Do you think I'm German?

IVANOVSKY. Excuse me, comrade?

TITOV. Gherman, German. Is that what you think?

IVANOVSKY. You're from Volgograd aren't you, comrade?

KOROLYOV (*into microphone*). Nearly there, Yuri, sorry about
the wait, these idiots can't remember the launch sequence.

(*Turning to scream at his team.*) Well, is the hatch sealed or
not! One of you cretins must know! Someone must
remember how to read the signal!

GELADZE *enters and stands next to* TITOV.

TITOV. My father was a teacher.

GELADZE (*distracted*). Yes.

TITOV. Comrade Gagarin is the son of a tractor driver. So it's as it should be.

GELADZE. Exactly.

Comrade Chief Designer, excuse me, what's the delay?

TITOV. You technicians loved those dogs, didn't you?

GELADZE. I need to remain informed, as officer-in-command I need...

KOROLYOV. Oh, you brass-arsed prick! Will you shut up! Buzzing in my ear like a fly bloated on cow shit! Officer in command? I'll bust you back to sergeant if I have to! You and the ghost of Uncle fucking Joe! Shut up!

GELADZE. I am your commanding officer...!

KOROLYOV. Shut up! All of you! The only voice I want to hear is someone telling me the hatch is sealed!

IVANOVSKY. I read the hatch sealed now, SP.

KOROLYOV. Thank fuck for that!

(*Into microphone.*) You're on your way, Yuri.

YURI (*offstage*). Standing by.

IVANOVSKY (*over this*). Second cosmonaut stand down.

TITOV. Did you love the dogs, Comrade Ivanovsky?

He's being helped out of his suit.

IVANOVSKY. They were beautiful dogs. Gentle, loving dogs.

TITOV. It's no place to put a dog, a metal box, spinning round the Earth...

KOROLYOV. Tell me what I want to hear! Now!

MISHIN. Launch sequence engaged.

KOROLYOV. Fire engines.

MISHIN. Firing engines.

KOROLYOV. Launch.

A roar that becomes deafening. YURI *whoops and yells over it.*

YURI. Let's go.

A growing glow of light, blinding, the deafening roar, it dies away.

The TECHNICIANS *all stand with their backs to* TITOV, *still staring up.*

YURI *is hanging over them, looking down. The other* COSMONAUTS *gather round* TITOV.

TITOV. Did you feel that? I couldn't breathe. The noise shook the air out of my lungs…

LEONOV. What did you see?

KOMAROV. What did it look like?

TITOV. The engines fired… clamps came off, there were boulders flying through the air like leaves… the rocket swayed a bit as it rose…

LEONOV. Yes…

TITOV. And then it was… a furnace… then just a spark… it was…

IVANOVSKY. Portholes opening, Yuri.

YURI *gasps as he sees the world.*

Everyone looking up, YURI *reaching down.*

TITOV. It was beautiful.

YURI. I can see the Earth.

It's beautiful.

KOROLYOV, *unnoticed by anyone but* MISHIN, *is suffering a minor heart attack.*

MISHIN. Sergei? Are you alright?

KOROLYOV. I'm fine. I'm fine.

KOROLYOV *exits*.

YURI (*looking down at the Earth*). I feel good.

How are you?

Weightless now. It's good. It's not unpleasant at all. I like it.

The flight's continuing as it should, everything normal. Reception's excellent. I'm carrying out observations of the Earth... I can see clouds... sea... I can see everything! You can't believe how beautiful the world is. I can't believe it. It's so beautiful.

Scene Four

Beside the launch bunker.

The DOCTOR *is listening to* KOROLYOV*'s heart.*

DOCTOR. You've had a heart attack.

KOROLYOV. Don't talk shit.

DOCTOR. You've had a heart attack.

The OLD MAN *enters and sits close beside him, really close. Death touching him.*

KOROLYOV. I need to get back.

DOCTOR. You need to go to hospital.

KOROLYOV. There's nothing wrong with my heart, witch.

DOCTOR. It's weak.

KOROLYOV. Then fix it!

OLD MAN. Make something of yourself. Live a bit of life for me.

DOCTOR. I can give you pills.

You need to go for tests.

KOROLYOV. This didn't happen. No one will hear about this. There's nothing wrong with my heart.

DOCTOR. There is. And I'll tell them so.

KOROLYOV. They'll take the work away from me!

DOCTOR. What do I care?

KOROLYOV. Why else am I breathing their air?! You hear them? The dead? You're still listening?

I'm done listening.

Give me the pills and keep my secret or I'll send you back, witch...

DOCTOR. You can't...

KOROLYOV. This is my place. I say what happens here. If I say you're going back to work the Gulag, you'll go.

Go on. It's where you belong, sucking on the dark and making yourself fat on dying souls.

OLD MAN. A rocket is no memorial, is it, Sergei?

KOROLYOV. I'm done listening to them!

He pushes away from the OLD MAN.

You think the Americans have to fight their way clear of an army of dead to get above the Earth? You think they have all those bony hands holding onto their ankles when they try and fly upwards?

Fuck heart attacks.

Fuck the dead and fuck you. I'm taking us all up to the brightest sunlight there is and you will keep your mouth shut and watch me soar.

The OLD MAN *is exiting.*

Give me the pills and let me get back to work. There's a boy still up there.

Now let me bring him home.

YURI *above. The start of his descent. He's being buffeted violently. We hear* IVANOVSKY *on the microphone, very distant and distorted.*

YURI. The rear module is still attached. I'm still spinning.

IVANOVSKY. Say again, Lieutenant.

YURI. I'm spinning g-loads... fierce...

IVANOVSKY. We're losing signal.

YURI. Crackling... heat shield I think... crackling... getting hot...

IVANOVSKY *says something inaudible.*

Please repeat... please repeat... radio signal lost please repe...

Scene Five

Farmland on the banks of the river Volga.

ANNA, *a farmer in her fifties, is weeding her field of potatoes. Her daughter* RITA *is looking towards the horizon.*

ANNA (*head down over her work*). Can you see her?

RITA. No.

ANNA. Then go and find her.

There's a distant bang overhead. RITA *looks up.* ANNA *doesn't notice.*

That calf's going to run into the river one of these days. It's because she has dappled skin. Beautiful, like sunlight through leaves. The pretty ones never have any sense. She doesn't know she's just a milk cow, she thinks she's an explorer. She thinks she can run away on her little shining hooves and be the world's first dancing heifer. Isn't that right?

RITA. There's something in the sky.

ANNA. Is it a calf? No. Do we have flying cattle? No. I swear, Rita, get your eyes on the ground and stop daydreaming before I take a hoe to your head. Is your missing husband up

there? Is he flying back to take you off my hands again and
spare me the grief of listening to your daydreams? No.
You're stuck here so find that cow or get weeding.

RITA (*pointing up*). Look! Look! I thought it was a cloud but
it's falling. A silver flower... the size of a daisy... a saucer...
look, a shining wheel...

ANNA *looks up at last*.

ANNA. Parachutes! Parachutes! Oh, the bastards! Oh, Rita,
come here! It's the soldiers again! Get behind me! Darling,
come here! Get behind me!

RITA. It's a man!

ANNA. I'll kill you myself. Don't worry. They won't have you.
They won't have you, darling.

YURI *drops out of the sky on his parachute and lands a
short distance away. He whoops in delight, laughing,
bouncing in a victory dance*.

YURI. I'm here! Look at me! I'm back! Did you miss me! I'm
back!

ANNA. Get back!

(*Raising hoe*.) Leave us alone!

YURI. Sorry, sorry.

(*Pulling off his helmet*.) Don't be scared, look, it's just me,
Yuri, I'm here, I'm real, I'm human, I'm Russian. Look.

He moves closer, smiling in delight.

Look, it's just Yuri home again, see? Nothing to be scared of.
It's just me. What's your name?

ANNA *doesn't answer, still pointing the hoe threateningly*.

Oh, you're so scared! Don't be. Look at this face, am I going
to hurt you? Didn't you see me? Didn't you see what I just
did?

RITA. You fell from the top of the sky.

YURI. That's right! That's right! The top of the sky. The edge
of everything you've ever known and here I am back again!

ANNA. So where did you fall from? Outer space?

YURI. Yes! Yes! You don't believe it? You're going to have to start believing it! Ask me what it looked like...

(To RITA.) What's your name, sweetheart?

RITA. Rita.

YURI. Ask me what it looked like.

RITA. What did it look like?

YURI. It was beautiful. It was beautiful. It was so... there's no words, Rita, there's no words, you wouldn't believe me...

YAKOV, *another farmer in his fifties, runs on and stops, nervous, keeping his distance.*

(Seeing him.) Oh, here we go.

(Waving.) Hullo there! How are you? Come on, it's alright!

YAKOV *looks round for support, two other* FARMERS *come to cluster behind him.*

It's alright! Come on!

He walks towards them, grabbing their hands, shaking vigorously.

Hullo there, Yuri Gagarin, first man in space.

(Shaking hands all round.) Cosmonaut Yuri Gagarin, how are you? Good to meet you. Did you see me?

YAKOV. Did your plane crash, comrade?

FARMER. We saw it fall...

YURI. No one crashed! No one crashed. I've been to space and I'm home again... Anyone got a drink on them?

YAKOV. You've been to the Moon?

YURI. On my way, comrade. On my way. First café on the road out of town. Look, there's going to be truckloads of guys with big gold shoulders here any second... let's get out of here... let me buy you boys a drink.

YAKOV. Is it true?

FARMER. Can't be.

YURI. I'm here to prove it, the drinks are on the first man in space, you drinking, Rita?

ANNA. Stay where you are, Rita.

YAKOV. You flew to space in this?

He holds out the bit of metal he's carrying.

YURI. Oh shit… don't think you're supposed to pick bits up… oh, keep it, we've got other boats to sail to the stars in… it was a bumpy ride home… what's your name?

YAKOV. Yakov Lysenko.

YURI. It was a bumpy ride home, Yakov, hold onto that bit and you can weld it back onto the rest of the thing and go up yourself.

YAKOV. Me?

YURI. Why not?

YAKOV. Me go to the stars?

YURI. Hey, I just did it. Look at me! If Yuri did it, any one of you could. That's the future, that's the future, comrades, let's drink to it!

FARMER (*to* YAKOV). We could go to Tanya's.

YURI. Does Tanya have vodka?

FARMER (*it's a stupid question*). Well, of course, it's a bar.

YURI. Then let's go! Hurry up, boys! Come on…

A military escort headed by LEONOV *in full formal regalia is hurrying towards them.*

Aw too late, never mind…

(*Waving and grinning.*) Alyosha! Shit, it's Alyosha! Over here!

YURI *and* LEONOV *grab each other in a hug.* YURI *breaks it and snaps a formal salute.*

USSR Cosmonaut Senior Lieutenant Gagarin reporting!

LEONOV (*grinning*). That's Major Gagarin now. They promoted you while you were up there.

YURI. Really?

(*To the* FARMERS.) Can you believe that?

Well, come here and give your superior officer some respect!

They grab each other in another hug, back-slapping.

You want to come up to Tanya's before the zoo starts? Me and these boys…

LEONOV. Yuri, Comrade Khrushchev is waiting to talk to you.

YURI. No… no!? You're joking. Shit, what am I going to say…?

LEONOV. What was it like up there?

YURI. We have to go now?

LEONOV. Yes! Tell me about the flight on the way. The car is waiting.

LEONOV *starts to lead* YURI *away.*

YURI. Well, can't someone get these boys a drink…

(*To the* FARMERS.) Look, wait there, just wait there, I'll do this and I'll nip back later… I'll see you later, alright?

(*As he exits with the escort.*) I'll see you later, Rita, see you, Yakov, I'll see you up there, yeah? The rest of you keep an eye on Cosmonaut Yakov! He's next! He's the man! I'll see you soon.

The FARMERS *stand, watching* YURI *go.*

ANNA. We'll see him again. On stamps. In statues.

YAKOV. I could be a cosmonaut.

ANNA. In your dreams.

YAKOV. He did it.

RITA. The smile he had…

ANNA *hits her.*

Scene Six

'Backstage' at the cenotaph in Red Square.

A terrified VALYA *is trying to nurse her baby.* KOROLYOV *watches.* YURI *and* KHRUSHCHEV *are out on the podium facing a roaring, cheering crowd that fills Red Square. They grin and wave, raising joined hands in a victory salute.*

KOROLYOV. All of Moscow's out there.

VALYA. Yes.

Aren't you going out there, Comrade Korolyov?

KOROLYOV. No. The chief designer has no face and no name. He's a secret weapon.

The news of this will have gone all round the world but none of my rivals in America have the smallest idea I even exist.

I'm hiding. It's a joke I play on them every day I'm working.

YURI *turns to them, grinning in delight.*

YURI. Valya! Come on, get out here!

VALYA. The baby, Yura!

(*Fussing with it.*) Oh, now I've upset her.

(*Soothing.*) Shhhh Shhhh...

KOROLYOV. I could hold her for you.

VALYA. No! No, I'm so sorry, she'll settle soon. I'm so sorry.

KOROLYOV. We're all unsettled.

VALYA. Yes.

KOROLYOV. You're a good mother.

VALYA. Thank you, comrade.

KOROLYOV. But this is all very stressful.

VALYA. I'm a nurse. I'm used to stress.

KOROLYOV. Life and death are easy; press conferences, however, take a bit of getting used to.

VALYA. This is an honour.

YURI. Valya!

KOROLYOV. It's alright. Let me hold the baby.

YURI. Come on!

KOROLYOV (*reaching for it*). It's fine, really.

VALYA *transfers the baby into his arms.*

VALYA. I am so sorry.

KOROLYOV. For what?

VALYA. It's very hard… all these eyes on you… but it's such an honour. Yuri's happy. He's so happy.

What am I supposed to do? What do they want me to do?

KOROLYOV. Just smile. And wave. They just want to see you.

(*Re: the crowd.*) I've never known anything like it. No one organised them. They just came.

VALYA. Why? What are they staring at! He's a man. He has arms and legs like them. His have just travelled a bit further. What do they want to look at?

KOROLYOV. Aren't you proud of him?

VALYA (*close to tears*). Of course I'm proud of him! He could have died! No one's done what he's done. But we need to go home. None of us can settle in this.

KOROLYOV *has settled the baby.*

(*Smiling in recognition.*) You've got children.

KOROLYOV. A daughter.

VALYA. Excuse me, Comrade Korolyov, for being so stupid. I'm standing here shaking and I've held a man's heart in my hands… I mean a bleeding one, a real one… hot and fluttering and I pressed it and pressed it and kept his life beating and I wasn't scared.

I can do better than this.

KOROLYOV. They won't see your hands shaking. Just wave and smile.

VALYA. It's an honour. It's just unexpected.

KOROLYOV. I know.

VALYA. You're right. He's still my Yura, isn't he? They all look at him but he doesn't change. He's made of strong metal. He just is who he is.

VALYA *walks out to stand beside* YURI *and* KHRUSHCHEV. YURI *hugs her then raises her arm to the crowd.*

YURI (*into microphone*). Glory to the Communist Party of the Soviet Union and our leader Nikita Sergeyevich Khrushchev!

A huge roar from the crowd.

KOROLYOV *walks up and down talking nonsense to the baby.*

KHRUSHCHEV. True Communism! Universal Communism is just around the corner!

GELADZE *enters quietly and watches him for a moment.*

GELADZE. Congratulations, Comrade Chief Designer.

KOROLYOV *looks round, startled.*

KOROLYOV. Thank you.

GELADZE. I had a question.

KOROLYOV. Yes?

GELADZE. You say the Vostok capsules can't be used as spy satellites…

KOROLYOV (*impatient*). I told you, we have to develop our capability to send men into space before we refine any defence application…

GELADZE (*cutting him off*). Why?

KOROLYOV. I've made my reports. I've made ten, twelve reports, books of figures, an encyclopaedia of notes. What is it that you don't understand this time, comrade?

GELADZE. How you've fooled us.

Pause. Stand-off.

KHRUSHCHEV *is shouting triumphantly from the balcony.*

KHRUSHCHEV. First man in space! First in the world! We're winning now! We're winning!

GELADZE. I've got another question for you, comrade.

Do you really think that Uncle Joe is dead?

Pause.

My father had no tips to his fingers, you know. Raw stumps like chewed sausage that bled clear water when the cold came every winter. Because he'd had to scrape the frozen ground with no hoe when the farmers turned him off the land. Because he'd had to eat weeds in a winter ditch. He lost his fingers. He was so ashamed of his hands.

Comrade Stalin rounded up all the farmers getting fat on the people's earth and he shot every greedy one of the fuckers.

Comrade Stalin taught us that all the weak hands, the broken fingers, all the starved and wounded muscles joined together, working together were stronger than iron.

Comrade Stalin gave my father his pride back. And that is the strength of Uncle Joe! You think a spirit like that could die with its father?

KOROLYOV. The defence of this country is always my priority, I've never neglected it.

GELADZE. What do you think you can do without the iron arms of the people to push your work forward? Any work that depends on the brain of one little man will weaken and fail in the end. Comrade Stalin wouldn't have let that happen. Those of us who remember him won't let it happen, Comrade Chief Designer.

KHRUSHCHEV. They can't catch us! They can't catch us now!

GELADZE. I can't catch you, comrade. Stupid of me.

Must try harder.

End of Act Two.

ACT THREE

Scene One

KHRUSHCHEV *addressing the United Nations.*

KHRUSHCHEV. So President Kennedy has made his speech. Not here. He won't come and talk to any of the rest of us. But we've all heard him, haven't we?

He doesn't like the way we're helping our friends in Cuba. Is that it? If our friends ask us to stand beside them, if they ask us for missiles, why shouldn't we help them? Cuba is an independent nation, Cuba is not your front doorstep, Mr Kennedy, whatever you'd like to believe.

So, right after Kennedy delivered his speech, I spoke with the US envoy, McCloy. We had a long conversation, talking about disarmament, but he wouldn't get to the point. So I said, 'Come to my place on the Black Sea tomorrow and we'll keep talking.'

On the first day before we talked we followed a Roman rite, we took a swim in my pool. I have my arm round this man and BANG, a camera goes off! Who is he going to show this picture to? Me in a Soviet pool with my arm round a man from Wall Street?! What is he playing at there? Eh!? How can I trust these people when they play tricks like that?

I said to him, 'I don't understand what sort of disarmament we can talk about, when your President Kennedy has already made this speech laying out his conditions and declaring war. What can I say? Please tell your president that we understand his terms, we accept his ultimatum and we'll respond in kind.'

And he's going... oh no... Kennedy didn't mean it, he meant to negotiate. He ummed and aahed but there was no point to any of it.

'You want to frighten us,' I said. 'You convinced yourself that Khrushchev will never go to war... so you scare us, expecting us to retreat. You're right, we'll not declare war, but we will not withdraw either.'

And I tell you now, if Kennedy wants a fucking war we'll shove one right up his arse! We're all big boys now aren't we? We wear long trousers, not short ones. I don't believe there'll be war. What am I counting on? I believe in your Western leaders' common sense. Because if a war starts, there will not be a stone left standing in the world!

War between the USSR and the United States would be a duel of ballistic intercontinental missiles. And there's our strength. America can't start a war with these weapons. They know it. They admit it. We have the advantage there!

Of course we're running a risk. But it has to be done. Lenin took a risk like this in 1917 when he said he had a party that could seize power. Everybody just smirked and snorted then... but look at us now!

We are not afraid of war, Mr Kennedy! The Soviet people are strong. You cannot frighten us! We are not afraid!

Scene Two

The DESIGN ENGINEERS' *room.*

KOROLYOV *and* NATASHA *are waiting.* NATASHA *is waiting to leave.* KOROLYOV *is waiting for the phone to ring, he's doing paperwork.*

NATASHA. Father, listen... it's been decided. I'm going to finish my medical degree.

KOROLYOV (*distracted*). Good.

NATASHA. Good?

KOROLYOV. Isn't it good?

NATASHA. You said... last time I was here you said...

KOROLYOV. It doesn't matter, Natasha. As long as you're happy.

NATASHA. I didn't enjoy the engineering modules I took... I know I performed well but... in the end I couldn't see the point.

KOROLYOV. Ah.

NATASHA. The relevance.

KOROLYOV. The relevance. I see.

NATASHA. The world will always need doctors, Dad.

KOROLYOV. Some doctors, yes.

NATASHA. But it won't always need rocket engineers.

KOROLYOV. How do you know? Maybe we'll all be living in the stars when you're my age.

NATASHA. Why would we want to do that?

KOROLYOV. Why not?

NATASHA. There's no air and it's too cold.

KOROLYOV. But think of the view.

GLUSHKO *enters*.

GLUSHKO. Anything?

KOROLYOV *shakes his head*.

NATASHA. Why hasn't the car come to take me back?

KOROLYOV. It's difficult tonight. There might not be any more cars tonight.

NATASHA. Why not?

KOROLYOV. Oh, we're on standby. Essential travel only.

NATASHA. Why?

KOROLYOV. Just one of those nights. You know how it is.

GLUSHKO. It's fine. There's nothing to worry about. There's no need to be frightened. Everything's going to be fine.

NATASHA. Why should I be frightened?

KOROLYOV. Thank you, Comrade Glushko.

NATASHA. Why should I be frightened?

GLUSHKO. Why did you bring her into the workroom?

KOROLYOV. This is the only phone line that works.

GLUSHKO. So, Natasha, have you enjoyed your visit to your father's empire?

NATASHA. It's... very interesting.

GLUSHKO. Interesting? Yes.

KOROLYOV. Stay. You don't need a car. Stay tonight. Stay the week. Nina would love to...

NATASHA. No!

No, I can't meet her.

Pause.

KOROLYOV. Your mother asked for the divorce. I didn't want that.

NATASHA. I know. But don't ask me to... I can't meet your new wife. Tell her I'm sorry. Tell her I had to go home.

KOROLYOV. As soon as we can get you a car.

Pause.

GLUSHKO. It's night in America now too.

If anything was going to happen it would have happened by now.

KOROLYOV. Oh, there's still time.

GLUSHKO. If anything was to...

(*Cautious of* NATASHA.) ...was to launch towards a terrestrial target then we would have heard. They'd have to prepare a launch pad.

KOROLYOV. They rang from Baikonur an hour ago. We had the probe ready to go to Mars. They told us to clear the launch pad and make way for an R16 missile. They're moving my rocket out of its way now.

Pause.

GLUSHKO. We should have more launch pads.

KOROLYOV. Well… yes. It's a tough choice, isn't it? Touch the stars or defend the motherland.

GLUSHKO. Years of impossible choices! No one could be expected to work to our targets. A demand is made and they want me to deliver it before they've finished speaking. It's too much. There's been too much impatience around the whole missile programme.

KOROLYOV *laughs*.

What's the joke?

NATASHA. What's the joke?

KOROLYOV. Seems Uncle Valentin likes to blow on his soup these days. Maybe he burnt his mouth too often sticking his spoon straight in the pot.

GLUSHKO. You cut corners too. You've just been lucky.

KOROLYOV. Glushko, you have your little kingdom and I have mine. Keep your greedy eyes off what I do and we'll say no more about your tragedies.

GLUSHKO. I've had no failures. None of my designs…

KOROLYOV (*cutting him off*). I knew that fuel system was a death trap. You must have known…

GLUSHKO. Your gambles have always paid off, that's the only difference between us.

KOROLYOV. Why do we have to push our short-range missiles into Cuba, Glushko?

GLUSHKO. You *cannot* talk about this!

KOROLYOV. What's happened to our long-range capability then? What's happened to all our missiles and those clever boys who thought they could fly even faster than me? Have you seen any of them around the place today?

GLUSHKO. I was *not* responsible for that design…

KOROLYOV. You sat down with the design team! You advised them. You let them pump poison through the engines!

Do you know what Uncle Valentin did, Natasha?

GLUSHKO. Sergei, you can't tell her this. What are you doing? What do you think you're doing?

KOROLYOV. A year ago, out in sunny Baikonur, where your old dad sweats and freezes and eats dust half the year, they put up a new missile for testing. Not my design, I'd given my opinion but they went ahead anyway... The fuel system was untried and lethal but Comrade Glushko approved.

GLUSHKO. You're mad!

KOROLYOV. Let's hope we can regret it tomorrow!

The rocket was leaking fuel on the launch pad. The cosmodrome commander was advised that it should be drained and made safe but that would have taken days... Everyone's impatient. He sent in ground staff to patch the leak... on a live rocket. The order was so insane no one knew how to deal with it.

GLUSHKO. Your hands are not clean, Sergei...

KOROLYOV. The boys went in... The launch sequence hadn't been cancelled properly. The first stage ignited...

A wall of flame swept out from the launch pad, a fire storm moving at a hundred kilometres a second. The ground crew tried to run on molten tarmac and burned where they fell... the commander fried where he sat watching...

A hundred and twenty lives, wasn't it? Do you know? Did you hear how many died, Valentin? I could never get a straight answer on that.

GLUSHKO. No one is to hear about it.

KOROLYOV. Oh, Valentin, to shout it out! Now! At last! Your madness meant our long-range missiles burnt along with the poor boys that built them. So now when America reaches out to squash us there's nothing the raving buffoon can do but stick his short range right up Kennedy's arse. So now we'll all burn.

NATASHA. Who's the raving buffoon?

GLUSHKO. So this week you're putting a poodle or a boy in the nose cone instead of a warhead... it doesn't mean you're flying doves, Sergei.

NATASHA. Who are you talking about? Who's the raving buffoon?

GLUSHKO. And you don't take risks. I put lives at risk to defend Mother Russia. You do it because you're crazy enough to think we can live in the sky and breathe without air.

KOROLYOV. I'm sorry, Natasha. We shouldn't fight like this in front of you.

NATASHA. I'm not an idiot. I know what you're talking about. There's going to be a war.

GLUSHKO. There's no such thing any more.

There's only an end.

That's why it won't happen.

KOROLYOV. What do you think will happen, Natasha?

NATASHA. We're told what will happen. The Soviet people will be victorious. Communism will unite all the struggling peoples of the world.

KOROLYOV. And what do you think will happen?

NATASHA. I think that might happen. Or I think the American capitalists might win.

GLUSHKO *sucks in his breath*.

I can say that. It's a possible outcome. We can't be afraid of imagining possible outcomes. That's the correct way to reach a successful diagnosis.

GLUSHKO. She's your daughter alright.

KOROLYOV. No, that's her mother. A mind like polished knives.

NATASHA. I don't think it'll happen, there are only a few capitalists in the world and there are a lot of workers. But we have to understand the capitalists could still win. We have to be ready.

KOROLYOV. And suppose neither side wins?

NATASHA. That's not possible.

KOROLYOV. Why not?

NATASHA. Because the fight has started.

KOROLYOV. Well… well, it's your future. It doesn't matter how I imagine it. You'll have to live it.

GLUSHKO. Pray she does.

KOROLYOV. I think she'll be living in the stars.

GLUSHKO. No you don't. No you don't! You're sitting there watching the seconds slide out of existence just like I am.

Pause.

All of Russia's asleep out there, farmers, factory workers… all sleeping. Lucky ignorant bastards.

Pause.

I made mistakes, Sergei. I admit it. They gave me no peace and they gave me no time. You think you'll never make a mistake? Why do you think they'll give you time?

KOROLYOV. Because we've already won. We can orbit the Earth for days, for seventy orbits. The American rockets can't even spin round it once.

GLUSHKO. You've won?

(*Laughs.*) You've won? Who told you the race was over, Sergei?

Pause.

They haven't rung.

KOROLYOV. Why would they ring?

I'm sorry you don't like Nina, Natasha.

NATASHA. Mother is… she has been very unhappy. She's still very unhappy.

KOROLYOV. I'm sorry. I didn't want that.

Nina is someone who helps me. She's someone I love.

But I love you too. You don't have to see her.

NATASHA. I don't think I can come here again.

KOROLYOV. You can visit again. I'll send Nina away. You can just visit me.

NATASHA. I don't think I can do that.

Pause.

KOROLYOV. Then I'm glad you're here now.

Scene Three

A resort by the Black Sea, outside.

Just LEONOV, *high above, looking down at the Earth. He's remembering.*

LEONOV. Then suddenly it became very quiet... I heard Pavel say, 'The lock's airtight, open the hatch...' I stared at the hatch. The lock loosened. The wheel turned and the hatch shook and opened... and there was all the sky there is... I was the first to see the billions of stars... not through a telescope, not from a spaceship... but just through the skin of my helmet. There are so many more stars than you can see from Earth... and they are so much brighter...

I thought... Alyosha, if you're a real cosmonaut you'll go outside now... I pushed up with both legs and there I was, on the edge of the airlock, in outer space.

Two television eyes followed my movement as if they were living creatures. The light... was the reflection of the Earth's atmosphere, the Earth turning below me like a majestic blue ball. And suddenly... you see that the Earth is round. You see that the atmosphere we breathe is a very thin layer. It's like tracing paper on a drawing. We have only twelve kilometres of oxygen above us when we walk on the Earth, just a skin of gas that makes our Earth blue. It was so silent. I could hear my breath and my heart beating. You think... We are a tiny grain of sand in this universe, but we are a grain of sand with brains. Because humanity, with all its ingenuity, sent me up here, I saw our Earth with the eyes of that grain of sand. I was able to do that.

LEONOV *is out of memory and back on Earth, surrounded by other* COSMONAUTS, YURI, TITOV, KOMAROV, *drinking, laughing, embracing him.*

YURI *pulls the glass out of* LEONOV*'s hand.*

YURI. Can you believe this clown was the first man to walk in space! He can't even find his own vodka glass.

KOMAROV. So he takes another man's drink.

YURI. No wonder Pavel came back down blue in the face. This greedy bastard was probably breathing his own oxygen and then sucking down all the rest!

LEONOV. Shut up and get me a drink!

YURI *puts one in his hand.*

YURI. I can't believe they let you go up there.

LEONOV. We all know the way now. It's easy. Straight up.

KOMAROV. Straight up past those American astronauts still trying to hold one orbit.

YURI. They are so beaten. They've crashed into our slipstream and they're tumbling like geese with broken wings. They know it.

(*Drinks.*) Victory to the cosmonauts of the Soviet people!

LEONOV. Poor American astronauts. If I met one up there I'd shake his hand.

YURI. I'd love to meet one of them. I'd hug him like a brother. Can you imagine it? Five minutes talking to one of those boys.

LEONOV. Get them all over here. That would be a party.

YURI. Just to compare the view. Because as it happens I know this boy's lying.

LEONOV. What?

YURI. Yeah, Comrade Artist, Comrade Poet with your sketchbook and your head banging off the stars. Have you heard him, Titov? Banging on about the 'beautiful sphere of the Earth?' You can't see the world's round! You can see a curve alright but...

LEONOV. No, no, I saw nearly the whole shape of it, curving away from me like...

YURI. You can't! The edge is halfway on your horizon like a bow...

LEONOV. No! I saw the sphere, I promise you, blue and silver and round...

TITOV (*cutting in*). He was higher up.

They were higher up than us, Yuri.

YURI. Of course. Of course that's it. That explains it.

TITOV. And they did so many more orbits. They had days to watch the Earth spinning below, to learn its shape.

YURI. Yeah. Right enough.

TITOV. I made seventeen orbits of the Earth. The light changed on every orbit. I remember every single one.

YURI. Yeah, apart from the orbits you slept through...

TITOV. It was part of the mission! I was supposed to test...

LEONOV (*over* TITOV). And the orbits when he was throwing up...

TITOV. Yes, but I suffered to save all the cosmonauts. We *discovered* low-gravity motion sickness because I experienced...

KOMAROV. Didn't he sleep through his alarm as well?

YURI. Half an hour the lazy bastard was snoring up there...

LEONOV. Second man in space. Snoozing and vomiting...

TITOV (*shouting them down*). Alright! Alright! Take another drink and shut up.

TITOV *tops them all up*.

KOMAROV. I can't believe they've never let you, either of you, meet the American astronauts. You must have shaken every other hand on the planet.

Didn't you kiss the Queen of England, Yuri?

YURI. Her hand, Komarov, her hand.

KOMAROV. So who was it you kissed?

YURI. I lost count.

TITOV. Gina Lollobrigida.

YURI. She was one of them.

TITOV. Did you see the Moon, Alyosha?

LEONOV. No. It was on the other side of the Earth.

YURI. I never saw it. I forgot to look.

KOMAROV. Next time.

YURI. Yes.

KOMAROV. I can't believe I'm launching again. What do you reckon, Yuri? Eighteen months?

TITOV. They've given you another flight?

KOMAROV. The new ship.

TITOV. I didn't know that.

YURI. No. We don't know that yet. Shut up, Komarov.

Where's the bottle? Cosmonaut, where have you put the bottle?

TITOV. But… Komarov has already had a mission… Yuri, the pilots were to be rotated.

YURI. No one ever said that.

TITOV. They did. It was agreed. Those of us who went first would go again.

YURI. And we will. I'm this loser's back-up. Look at the state of him, guaranteed to trip over his feet on the launch pad. Don't you worry, Gherman, we'll get our turn again.

VALYA *enters*.

VALYA. There's a woman waiting outside our room.

LEONOV. Valya Goryacheva, there you are, come and join us.

VALYA. It's late.

   She won't go away, Yuri. She moved to the end of the corridor. She's just sitting there. Waiting.

YURI. Well, what does she want?

VALYA. She won't tell me.

YURI. So tell her to go away.

VALYA. She says she's a doctor.

YURI. What do you mean, 'She says she's a doctor'?

VALYA. That's what she says.

YURI. So the doctors want to stick their needles in me again. Tell her to wait till tomorrow. The first cosmonaut's busy.

VALYA. I'm not talking to her again.

YURI. So ignore her. Go to sleep.

   Valya, come and have a drink or go to bed!

   VALYA *exits*.

LEONOV. Those doctors never leave you alone, do they?

TITOV (*sarcastic*). Doctors and film stars, we've got a tough life, eh, Yuri? These fledgling cosmonauts have no idea what it was like to go first.

   YURI *says nothing*.

KOMAROV. The Moon's risen over the roof, look.

   You know, I can't always believe I've been up there.

LEONOV. Right there…

   Looking down on the Black Sea…

KOMAROV. I couldn't believe I was going up the first time. When did it seem real to you?

YURI. It never did. Because right up to the moment we took off I still thought Titov would be going instead of me.

TITOV. So did I.

This is the first time this has been said. They look at each other, then burst into roars of laughter, bear hugs.

The Queen of England? Was that the best you could do?

YURI. At least I got a live one. You shake hands with the President of America and then they shoot him in the head.

TITOV. I liked him. He looked you straight in the eyes. Good handshake.

KHRUSHCHEV *and* BREZHNEV *enter.*

KHRUSHCHEV. He was a shifty little fucker. Sweaty palms. Didn't you feel his clammy little palm?

All the COSMONAUTS *are scrambling to attention.*

LEONOV. Comrade First Secretary… we didn't know… Excuse us…

KHRUSHCHEV. Boys! Boys! What are you doing? Yuri, what are you doing? Come here! Come on!

He holds out his arms, embraces YURI.

Oh, Yuri Alexeyevich, it's good to see you. Are you pissed yet?

YURI. On my way, comrade.

KHRUSHCHEV. Good man. Good man, let's have some more.

KHRUSHCHEV *is already drunk.* BREZHNEV *is not.* BREZHNEV *stays back, just watching* KHRUSHCHEV *and the* COSMONAUTS.

Drink! Drink! Come on. This is a holiday. How often do I get a holiday? How often does the humble First Secretary get to drink with the first men in space?

TITOV. We're honoured, First Secretary.

KHRUSHCHEV. Course you are but you're not nearly pissed enough. Hurry up, man, drink.

KOROLYOV *enters.*

Oh, here he is, the guest of honour, late for his own fucking party. Where have you been, Sergei Pavlovich?

YURI. Hey! Just in time. Grab a glass, Comrade Chief Designer.

TITOV. Like he'll take a drink.

KOMAROV. Are you alright, comrade?

KOROLYOV. Too many people with nothing better to do than delay me and annoy me. I'm here now. Nikita Sergeyevich, we didn't expect you

KHRUSHCHEV. Well, here I am, I came all this way to see you, Sergei. To discuss things with you. To review your progress.

Just an informal chat. While we're all relaxing in this beautiful place. Isn't it beautiful?

KOROLYOV. Yes.

KHRUSHCHEV. Clean air, a sea like a dark sparkling wheatfield tossed by the night breeze…

Paradise. We live in paradise. That's what you boys deserve. My warriors with wings. You've soared up into that night sky…

…and shat on the White House. Oh yes. Oh yes, you've showed them.

We've showed them everything now! We've showed them we can out-think them, we've showed them we can beat them into space, we've showed them we can operate strategically…

Isn't that right?

Well, isn't it!?

ALL. Yes, Comrade First Secretary.

KHRUSHCHEV (*to* BREZHNEV). Isn't that right, Comrade Deputy?

He's not saying anything. He's not in the mood for conversation.

I don't know what's got into him. Something is up. Eh?

You're starting to get on my nerves, comrade! Voice an opinion. Share your thoughts. Go on.

BREZHNEV *says nothing. He is getting out some paperwork.*

There were missiles in Turkey. He had his little toy rockets in Turkey! Who made him take them down? I did! I did! Don't tell me I blinked first! I take them out of Cuba, he scurries out of Turkey! He blinked! Not me! Why are they saying I blinked!

The world will see soon! The world will see who really has the upper hand!

(*To* BREZHNEV.) You tell them! Why else are you standing there!

BREZHNEV (*offering papers*). Comrade Khrushchev, I'm afraid this requires your urgent attention.

KHRUSHCHEV. Oh, let me drink in peace, will you!?

(*Raising glass.*) The world united behind the Soviet people!

They all drink.

(*Re: his drink.*) Fuck, I'm not feeling that... is this the good stuff?

Good enough, eh? Good enough for you, eh, Comrade Chief Designer. What's your latest plan then, tell me, when are we going to have another triumph to show the world? The first man in space, the second man in space, the first two-man mission, the first woman, the first space walk... drink, drink, Comrade Leonov... What's on the launch pad after that?

KOROLYOV. The next launch is our latest probe to Mars, comrade, we hope...

KHRUSHCHEV (*cutting him off*). And why the fuck are we going to Mars!!

KOROLYOV *doesn't answer.*

Drink, drink, drink, come on, come on, we're having a conversation here.

KOROLYOV *takes a sip.*

(*To* LEONOV.) Do you want to go to Mars?

LEONOV. Eh... if you want to send me, Comrade Khrushchev.

KHRUSHCHEV (*laughing*). Listen to him! I love this boy. Where is Mars? Point to it. Look, look up there. The whole sky over the Black Sea. Point to Mars.

LEONOV *hesitates*.

Alright, so point to the Moon.

LEONOV *does so instantly*.

You see my point, Comrade Chief Designer.

Let's aim for something we can fucking see!

KOROLYOV. Our scientific probes to Mars and Venus are exceeding any attempt by the Americans to match...

KHRUSHCHEV. Because they're not fucking trying to get to Mars, are they!? They don't care if we go there, do they? We can run away and lose ourselves in the darkest corners of the sky and they'll wave us on our way!

Sergei. Dear Sergei. I love you. You know I do. Come here.

He embraces KOROLYOV.

We need to keep astonishing them, Sergei. The magic. Another first. Take us to the Moon, Sergei. No one cares about Mars.

BREZHNEV. What became of your Mars probe, Comrade Korolyov?

The last one.

Pause.

KOROLYOV. It blew up shortly after take-off.

BREZHNEV. I don't think the people can be asked to make expensive sacrifices for technology that doesn't even work.

BREZHNEV *is offering papers again*.

KHRUSHCHEV. Exactly, comrade.

You heard him. He doesn't say much, but when he opens his mouth at least it fucking makes sense.

KHRUSHCHEV *signs*.

BREZHNEV. This is excellent vodka, comrade.

KHRUSHCHEV. It is the good stuff, isn't it? Well done. Let me top you up.

BREZHNEV (*taking back papers*). Just a little, comrade. There's a lot of work to be done tonight.

KHRUSHCHEV. Is there? I thought we were on holiday?

BREZHNEV. Honoured cosmonauts, you'll have to excuse the First Secretary. He's very tired.

KHRUSHCHEV. No I'm fucking not.

BREZHNEV. There's still business to be done here tonight.

KHRUSHCHEV. No there fucking isn't! Boys! Yuri! Come on, we're having a party.

The COSMONAUTS *are exiting.*

KOMAROV. Goodnight, comrades.

LEONOV. Goodnight, Comrade First Secretary.

YURI. Goodnight, Nikita Sergeyevich. Don't work too hard. Look after yourself.

They exit.

KHRUSHCHEV. What the fuck did you do that for?

BREZHNEV. Nikita Sergeyevich, you are very tired.

KHRUSHCHEV. I keep telling you! I'm not tired!

BREZHNEV. No one could have done more for the people.

No one would deny you your retirement. You've earned it, Nikita.

KHRUSHCHEV. What are you talking about?

BREZHNEV. The Politburo agrees.

KHRUSHCHEV. Agrees with what?

BREZHNEV. No one expects one man to lead our great nation through so many difficult years. Only Comrade Stalin could do that. We should never ask anyone to try and fill the place of Comrade Stalin.

The Politburo have asked me to tell you they understand how great a burden you've borne for us all. The people thank you.

Holds up papers.

In sorrow but with gratitude we accept your decision to stand down from office.

To show our appreciation the people have built you another lovely dacha, only five miles from here.

It's a beautiful spot, Nikita. The views are superb. A car is waiting to take you there now.

Pause.

KHRUSHCHEV. Always at my shoulder. Like a statue. Watching everything with your stone eyes.

BREZHNEV. It was my privilege, Comrade Khrushchev.

KHRUSHCHEV *slowly starts to exit.*

BREZHNEV. You can take the bottle.

KHRUSHCHEV. Fuck you.

KHRUSHCHEV *exits.*

BREZHNEV. 'If Kennedy wants a fucking war we'll shove one right up his arse.'

That was my favourite quote.

Shouted in the United Nations. The translators didn't convey 'fucking' of course but everyone understood the word 'arse'.

KOROLYOV. If you'll excuse me, Comrade Brezhnev.

BREZHNEV. I'm afraid not, comrade. Our work's not over.

This way.

BREZHNEV *ushers* KOROLYOV *off.*

Scene Four

A bedroom at the Black Sea resort.

YURI *is starting to undress, impatient. The* DOCTOR *stands watching.*

DOCTOR. Comrade Major...

YURI. Oh fuck, if you're going to look at my cock, call me Yuri.

DOCTOR. Yuri...

You saw a young woman. A nurse at Star City a few weeks ago.

YURI *instantly tenses up.*

YURI. What about her?

DOCTOR (*gentle*). I like Anya very much. She works with me sometimes. She's good fun but she's not very clever.

She has an infection.

She told me that she might have given it to you.

I know your family arrived today, Major, so I thought I should speak to you as soon as possible.

YURI. Oh fuck... Oh fuck...

YURI *starts to cry. The* DOCTOR *hesitates then she goes to hold him gently.*

I'm sorry... I'm so sorry... I'm just drunk... I'm sorry.

DOCTOR. It's alright. It's alright.

YURI. They won't let me fly! What am I supposed to... (*Nearly breaking down again.*)

DOCTOR. Just breathe slowly, that's it.

YURI (*calming himself*). They won't let me fly. I wanted to fly down here... they only had the latest MiG... they said... they said I didn't have enough flying hours... I didn't understand the new instrument panel... they've kept me out of the air so long I've forgotten how to fly!

DOCTOR. Well... the first cosmonaut is an important man. They can't risk him to a bit of turbulence.

YURI. I'm a pilot! That's what I am!

They put me in passenger planes. They fly me all round the world, waving and smiling, waving and smiling...

DOCTOR. You have a very good smile. It's been very effective travelling the world...

YURI. And Valya... Oh, Valya...

She hates it. She hates it. The flying. The bouquets of flowers. The drinks. The photographs. She hates it all. She's so shy, you know... it's like they're torturing her, dragging her out, forcing her to stand beside me, waving at the world.

I'm supposed to make her happy. But she never smiles any more.

VALYA *enters. She steps back as she sees them, listening. They don't see her.*

I put my foot down. I said, 'Don't do this to her. Let her stay home with her work, with the babies. Come on! Leave her alone!'

And she's still not...

She says I've changed. She says I'm never there... I never was there! I'm a pilot! She says I just want to talk to big shots and women in low dresses... I have to talk to them! I have to smile at them! They come up to me, hundreds of hands, hundreds of smiles... 'Major Gagarin, just let me shake your hand, just let me touch you, it'd make me so happy.'

Anya was... Anya was happy anyway. She'd've fucked me even if I wasn't a hero of the Soviet people, she just...

She was just easy. And she smiled.

VALYA *walks forward.* YURI *and* VALYA *just look at each other.* YURI *looks away.*

DOCTOR. Major Gagarin is in the middle of a medical examination.

VALYA. Have you checked his hands?

DOCTOR. I don't understand what you mean.

VALYA. Yuri does.

VALYA *exits*.

YURI *cuts the* DOCTOR *off, following* VALYA.

He exits.

After a moment the DOCTOR *follows.*

Scene Five

A reception room at the Black Sea resort.

BREZHNEV *ushers* KOROLYOV *on.*

KOROLYOV. What do you want to say to me?

BREZHNEV. All in good time, comrade, we're waiting.

KOROLYOV. What for?

BREZHNEV. For the members of the review board.

KOROLYOV. What review board?

BREZHNEV. Here they are.

GLUSHKO *and* GELADZE *enter.*

KOROLYOV. Oh, I see.

MISHIN *and* IVANOVSKY *enter.*

I see.

BREZHNEV. I've been observing your progress, Comrade Korolyov. These comrades have been observing your work.

KOROLYOV. Have they?

(*To* IVANOVSKY.) Oleg, don't worry, it's alright.

BREZHNEV. You're looking tired, Comrade Korolyov.

KOROLYOV. Oh, you think? Is that what you think? And you imagine you can have a space programme without me!?

BREZHNEV. The sole, tangible benefit of our space programme is propaganda. Our flights into space proved that Soviet workers lead the world. Our respected *former* chief secretary was right. The world doesn't care if you fly machines to Mars now. America has said they will land a man on the Moon. We need to get there first. We need a space programme solely focused on that goal.

KOROLYOV. So you want to destroy years of research, just give up on any practical idea of exploring the universe to plant a flag on the nearest lump of rock?

BREZHNEV. Has Comrade Korolyov's team remained within budget, General Geladze?

GELADZE. Never. He spends the sweat of our people on toys, then he comes back with his hand out asking for more.

BREZHNEV. Comrade Glushko?

GLUSHKO. I've observed an inefficient use of resources.

KOROLYOV. What resources? What resources? You want me to match the Americans with kites made of brown paper and glue!?

BREZHNEV. It's incorrect to state that the Americans are superior. If sufficient effort is made we will always succeed. That has been proven. But in these times, in *these* new times, comrade... every rouble must count. Is your team within budget, Comrade Glushko?

GLUSHKO. Yes.

KOROLYOV. You want to give my team to *him*?

BREZHNEV. Under our new economic measures the Politburo considers it is always more efficient to combine departments.

KOROLYOV. He's had his head up a missile's fuel pipe the last five years. You think he could even understand my calculations?

GELADZE. The people are not stupid, comrade!

The people could understand your intentions if they were explained correctly.

Comrade Korolyov does not respect the debt he owes to the Soviet people.

KOROLYOV. Oh, I respect that, Geladze, better than you. Better than you could ever understand...

(*To* BREZHNEV.) All the triumphs that amazed the world came from my work! Give me five years, comrade. Five more years. I'll get you back there.

BREZHNEV. No one is denying your achievements, comrade, but the people have placed too great a burden upon you. Those closest to you have observed that you have grown tired.

Comrade Mishin.

MISHIN. The Comrade Chief Designer works harder than any of us.

BREZHNEV. Which has worn him out.

MISHIN. He never stops. No one can match his effort.

BREZHNEV. He should not be asked to make such effort. Isn't that right, Comrade Ivanovsky?

If you thought his health was in danger, you yourself would beg him to stand aside, wouldn't you?

IVANOVSKY. He's never sick.

BREZHNEV. And he musn't become sick. We must protect him.

(*Calling off.*) Comrade Doctor.

The DOCTOR *enters.*

Comrade Doctor, the people thank you for giving testimony to this committee.

What is your opinion of Comrade Korolyov's health?

DOCTOR. It's... fragile. I asked to examine him tonight. I had observed certain... symptoms.

BREZHNEV. You've been treating him for some time?

DOCTOR. Yes.

BREZHNEV. For a heart condition?

DOCTOR. Yes.

BREZHNEV. And is it your opinion that his condition could affect his ability to work?

DOCTOR. Yes.

KOROLYOV. She's lying!

She doesn't know what she's talking about. She caught me a bit faint once, once…

Alright, I was weak, I let the silly cow put her hand on my brow, I was tired that day, that one day… she gives me a few pills… I took them… I'm not going to insult her profession…

DOCTOR. Comrade Korolyov has a weak heart…

KOROLYOV. Here they are! Look!

Takes out the bottle of pills.

The bottle's full! Look! I've barely touched them. Take them back.

Throws them at the DOCTOR.

I don't need them!

BREZHNEV. We can't risk your health, Sergei Pavlovich. Your skills are too rare, too precious. The people want you to stand aside. To share your burden. Between them, Comrade Glushko and General Geladze can…

KOROLYOV (*cuts him off*). Not a fucking chance!

BREZHNEV. I've had twenty years of his ranting, Sergei Pavlovich, but I won't suffer five minutes of yours. Shut your filthy mouth!

Beat.

You will be replaced as chief designer by Comrade Glushko and General Geladze will take over full supervision of the cosmonaut programme.

KOROLYOV. No.

BREZHNEV. We're not offering you a choice, Sergei Pavlovich.

KOROLYOV. Then you'll have no space programme.

> (*Indicating* GLUSHKO *and* GELADZE.) Ask them the results of the latest experiments our team have conducted on thermal exchange.

GELADZE. You're wasting our time, comrade.

KOROLYOV. We need to change to a bell-shaped heat shield, I have it in development. Ask them the most cost-effective route to bring the completed rocket parts to the launch site.

GLUSHKO. Sergei, stop this.

KOROLYOV. We can assemble them at the plant and then disassemble them for rail transport, I'll save you thousands of roubles every trip. Ask them the name of the secretary who types up the assembly instructions. Elena Savitskaya, if you smile at her she'll do the work of two women in half the time. I understand every part of this work, Comrade Brezhnev, and I move every part of it forward. You want to beat the Americans? You want to go to the Moon? The rocket I'm developing now will match anything the Americans are launching. My Soyuz is ready to go! It can be on the launch pad in eighteen months, I guarantee it!

BREZHNEV (*to* MISHIN). Is that correct?

MISHIN. We... we... our target was two years... to test a prototype...

KOROLYOV. We can do it, can't we, Oleg?

IVANOVSKY. We can do it, comrade. We won't sleep.

GELADZE. He sits behind his desk, dreaming of space and demanding that the party foots the bill for his fantasies! The people have been cheated for long enough, Comrade Brezhnev!

KOROLYOV. In eighteen months you could have another triumph, Comrade Brezhnev, but right now, if you want a working space programme you need me to run it. So how badly do you want a space programme?

BREZHNEV (*to* GLUSHKO). Can his next mission launch in eighteen months?

GLUSHKO (*to* KOROLYOV). You believe you can do that?

BREZHNEV (*to* GLUSHKO). He just said he could. I'm asking you if it's possible.

GLUSHKO (*still to* KOROLYOV). This is what you want, Sergei?

BREZHNEV. Comrade Glushko!

KOROLYOV. Tell him.

GLUSHKO. Comrade Korolyov has achieved many things that might have been considered impossible. He has never had to work to a deadline as tight as this, but if he says he can do it…

BREZHNEV. Yes or no?!

GLUSHKO. I'm certain no one else could. No one else would even try.

GELADZE. Comrade Korolyov cannot be trusted. We know he cannot be trusted.

BREZHNEV (*to* GELADZE). You read the latest intelligence on the American space programme.

GELADZE. The Americans are making fast progress, yes, but we can't allow that to frighten us.

BREZHNEV. This is not about fear, comrade. It's about results. Success is vital.

(*To* KOROLYOV.) It seems the people must ask you to labour a little longer, Comrade Chief Designer.

(*To* GELADZE.) The people deserve their dreams too, Comrade Geladze. I will trust you to monitor Comrade Korolyov closely.

GELADZE. Every second. Every rouble.

BREZHNEV (*to* KOROLYOV). Eighteen months, comrade.

BREZHNEV *and* GELADZE *exit.*

GLUSHKO. Now you're going to learn what it means to work faster. Eighteen months? Good luck.

GLUSHKO *exits.*

MISHIN. Sergei… I didn't know what to say…

KOROLYOV. It's fine, Vassily, you did fine. Go have a drink. Go on.

He hugs IVANOVSKY.

I knew you had tears in there somewhere. Don't waste them, Oleg. It's fine. We're winning again. Go on.

IVANOVSKY. Aren't you coming, Sergei?

KOROLYOV. In a minute. I need some fresh air.

IVANOVSKY *and* MISHIN *exit.*

KOROLYOV *stands looking at the* DOCTOR *for a moment then he moves away. The* DOCTOR *follows him.*

Scene Six

The Black Sea resort, outside.

KOROLYOV *walks out, looking out over the sea. He's in pain.*

The DOCTOR *follows him.*

DOCTOR. You ruined him.

KOROLYOV. What are you talking about?

DOCTOR. You picked up Major Gagarin like a piece of wet mud and you rolled your fingerprints all over him and then you crumbled him and threw him away.

KOROLYOV. Oh, is that why? That's why you tried to bomb us back to smoke and rubble. I was right, wasn't I? The frostbitten old hag's just another girl who wants to kiss a cosmonaut. Lovely.

DOCTOR. I just tried to save your life. Again.

KOROLYOV. Take your hands off my life! Get your evil bony
    fingers out of my heart.

DOCTOR. You're having an attack now. Aren't you?

KOROLYOV. It won't kill me.

DOCTOR. It might. Do you want your pills?

KOROLYOV. Leave me alone.

DOCTOR. They know anyway. Take your pills.

KOROLYOV. Get away from me.

DOCTOR. You think I'll just stand here and watch you die?
    You think I'd let that happen?

    You're right.

    I might. This time I just might.

KOROLYOV. I won't die.

DOCTOR. You think? How does that work?

KOROLYOV. I don't choose to die yet.

DOCTOR. Oh, that's how it works. The great Korolyov, with
    his own will he defeats death and rules the skies.

    My God, look at that sky.

    (*Looking up.*) Do you know the name of every star?

KOROLYOV. No.

DOCTOR. No? So you fire them up there, but you don't even
    know where you're sending them.

KOROLYOV. We've hardly started.

DOCTOR. No time to draw star maps.

KOROLYOV. Five years, that's all I need.

DOCTOR. 'Just one more day, just one more day, please,
    please, just a little more life. You'll see, you'll see how
    important my life is if you just give me one... more...
    day...' And you don't even believe in prayer, Sergei.

    You think you are God. But look, you really are dying.

She holds out the pills.

Here. Come and get them.

KOROLYOV *tries to reach her.*

They might not save you even if you make it. It's a gamble.
It's fifty-fifty but that's alright, isn't it? You can live with
those odds.

KOROLYOV *is still trying to reach her.*

Seventy-thirty.

You've nothing, have you? No name. No fame...

Eighty-twenty. Your chest's closing down. No family to cry
over you. No one to stroke your picture on a stone. Look at
you. That's some dream you're fighting to live for, Sergei.

He collapses.

After a moment she goes to him. Puts pills in his mouth.

Back of your tongue. Breathe. Breathe, that's it.

She gets an injection ready.

I read your figures once. Forbidden paper left out on the
desk. The bill for just one of your toys. All those zeros. All
those roubles.

Enough to buy every little girl in the Soviet Republics two
pairs of sandals and a bowl of chicken soup every day of her
life.

That's all I wanted. When I was a little girl. I don't suppose
the little girls who've grown up with your metal toys whizzing
over their heads are so different. Or we could keep them free
of measles, polio... let them skip in those sandals. What do
you think? But of course you're just doing the best job you
can. The orders come from somewhere else. The roubles
aren't yours to spend anyway. Is that what you'd like to say? If
you had breath to speak? Just because you think the dream's
worth dying for, Sergei, it doesn't mean the dead agree.

She injects him. KOROLYOV *goes still.*

It is such a beautiful night.

I'd forgotten there were nights like this. A wind that doesn't
strip the skin off your face.

A sky that's warm and black. Just one slice of Moon. Frosty
watermelon. Oh… wouldn't you kill for fresh watermelon.
You see you can tell me those are huge suns blazing up there.
You can tell me their light is older than dead gods and the
dark between them is centuries wide… But I just see a tent
of summer night, sparkling over my head. What's wrong
with sparkles, why can't you let me imagine twinkling
candles up there in the dark? What comfort did you ever
imagine you'd get looking into eternity, Sergei?

KOROLYOV. When I saw your little face… the terror on it
when they fired the first shot. I saw you shatter, as I had…
when I understood that nothing could save me and they'd
thrown me in hell. Prisoners, guards, doctors… we were all
in hell. Oh my God, darling, you were just a girl. They'll
never pay for what they did to you. They should rot in hell
for what they did to you. I don't hate you… It wasn't your
fault. You were a scared girl. We were all broken there. All of
us. I never believed it was your fault.

What is it?

Are you crying?

DOCTOR. I can't. Everything is dry.

KOROLYOV. I know.

Keep me alive a little longer.

DOCTOR. That's my job. If I have the means to do it. I've a
cupboard full of pills now.

But I still don't have an apartment.

KOROLYOV. I tried.

DOCTOR. Did you really? And you can reach up with your
metal hands and touch the Moon.

KOROLYOV. Forgive me.

DOCTOR. On a night like this, don't you think to want more
than the air around you is just greedy?

Stay there.

KOROLYOV *tries to get up.*

Stay still, Sergei.

It's time to stop.

It's time to sit and just look up at the sky and leave it alone.

KOROLYOV. No. I won't lie down.

DOCTOR. I'll get you a fucking wheelchair then.

KOROLYOV. No...

DOCTOR. Take some help, Sergei! Come on! No one will see.

She helps him to sit.

KOROLYOV. Are you still sorry that you saved me?

DOCTOR. What does any of that mean?

The DOCTOR *exits.* KOROLYOV *looks at the sky.*

TITOV *enters carrying a suitcase.*

TITOV. Goodbye, Comrade Chief Designer.

KOROLYOV. You're leaving, Lieutenant?

TITOV. I'm rested enough. I want to get back to Star City.

KOROLYOV. Alright.

TITOV (*notices* KOROLYOV's *condition*). Are you alright,
Sergei Pavlovich?

KOROLYOV. Of course... of course... just... looking at the sky.

Safe journey, cosmonaut.

KOROLYOV *looks back at the sky.* TITOV *hesitates.*

TITOV. Comrade Chief Designer, you oversee every part of our
space programme.

KOROLYOV. Oh yes. I still do that.

TITOV. Are the cosmonauts to be rotated? Will those who were
first be useful again?

KOROLYOV. You're always useful, Gherman.

TITOV. I was the most outstanding pilot in the whole of the Soviet Republics.

KOROLYOV. That's well known, Titov.

TITOV. I was the best.

I was the second cosmonaut. I was up there. Now I'm planted back in the earth.

That's the truth, isn't it?

I'm just one of the eight billion people on this Earth who'll never touch the Moon.

KOROLYOV. What will you do now?

TITOV. I'll find another ambition, Sergei Pavlovich.

KOROLYOV. Good luck.

TITOV. Thank you.

TITOV *exits*.

KOROLYOV. But the race has to be run to the end.

Scene Seven

The Chief Designer's room.

IVANOVSKY *and* MISHIN *are listening to a radio signal. It's the live feed from an American Gemini mission.* SCHIRRA *and* STAFFORD *are in Gemini 7,* BORMAN *and* LOVELL *in Gemini 6. They are attempting the first space rendezvous of two vessels.*

The signal should be crackly and indistinct, but audible.

SCHIRRA (*on radio*). You got a visual on that, Tom?

STAFFORD (*on radio*). No sign yet.

BORMAN (*on radio*). Steady on the radar, Tom.

STAFFORD (*on radio*). Copy that, Frank.

BORMAN (*on radio*). What's the view like?

SCHIRRA (*on radio*). Houston, this is Gemini 6, are you reading us?

STAFFORD (*on radio*). There's light cloud cover over most of Asia... I can see... brownish land mass just below us now... looking up towards... guess that's Siberia... can see a great stretch of white... leading up to the polar ice caps there...

SCHIRRA (*on radio*). Houston, this is Gemini 6?

STAFFORD (*on radio*). Got to catch us soon, just coming over the curve. I'm reading Gemini 7 ahead.

LOVELL (*on radio*). Roger that, Tom. We see you.

BORMAN (*on radio*). I tell you after three days up here I'm ready for some company.

SCHIRRA (*on radio*). Cutting thrusters...

STAFFORD (*on radio*). Copy that...

And I've got visual on Gemini 7. How you doing, John?

LOVELL (*on radio*). Do you guys want to hurry it up a little? I can't hold this parking spot for ever you know.

STAFFORD (*on radio*, *laughs*). Roger that.

KOROLYOV *enters*. IVANOVSKY *turns to him*.

IVANOVSKY. You're missing it.

KOROLYOV. How are they?

MISHIN. The two vessels are within sight of each other. They're attempting the rendezvous.

KOROLYOV. How far?

IVANOVSKY. I don't know. I can't understand everything.

SCHIRRA (*on radio*, *under this*). On approach.

LOVELL (*on radio*). Looking good, Gemini 6.

SCHIRRA (*on radio*). Don't want to scratch the paintwork.

LOVELL (*on radio*). Houston, this is Gemini 7... I have Gemini 6 on approach, do you copy?

STAFFORD (*on radio*). No one listening.

KOROLYOV. We can hear you, astronaut. Good luck.

MISHIN. They're still out of range of their ground station.

KOROLYOV. Yes. No one listening but us.

LOVELL (*on radio*). Still looking good, Gemini 6.

BORMAN (*on radio*). I've got our speed at twenty-eight thousand.

SCHIRRA (*on radio*). Copy that…

IVANOVSKY. Are they going to overshoot?

MISHIN. I can't hear…

IVANOVSKY. What's their speed? There's a collision risk?

KOROLYOV. They're steady.

IVANOVSKY. This is worse than having our boys up there. No instrument feed… nothing we can do…

MISHIN. Drive straight, Americans. Keep it steady.

STAFFORD (*on radio*). Six hundred metres… five hundred… four hundred…

IVANOVSKY. Slow it down!

STAFFORD (*on radio*). Three hundred… two hundred…

Long pause.

IVANOVSKY. What's happening?

MISHIN. Come on… come on, America… talk to us…

A louder clearer radio voice. Mission Control.

MISSION CONTROL (*on radio*). Gemini 6, this is Houston… do you copy?

Silence.

Gemini 7… Houston to Gemini 7… come in, John…

Silence.

MISHIN. They collided. They were going too fast.

MISSION CONTROL (*on radio*). Gemini 6…

A crackle as the fainter radio signal returns.

STAFFORD. Houston, this is Gemini 6… We are thirty-six metres apart and sitting…

An uproar of cheering on the radio from Houston. IVANOVSKY, MISHIN and KOROLYOV are slapping each other on the back, delighted.

IVANOVSKY. They did it!

MISSION CONTROL (*on radio*). Copy that… We'd have been happy with six hundred, Gemini 6… Congratulations… That's a world first!

The signal starts to break up. KOROLYOV bangs the radio. As the voice returns he bangs it harder.

I think we can tell the folks we're on our way to the Moon now…! That the world's first space rendezvous… Gemini 6 and 7, you are looking good!

KOROLYOV *bangs again and the radio dies. Their elation has died rapidly.*

They look at each other.

IVANOVSKY (*completely different tone*). They did it.

KOROLYOV. Yes.

MISHIN. We thought you were going to miss it.

KOROLYOV. The committee wanted a detailed report.

And on the way back there was a fucking cow on the road.

MISHIN. Again!

KOROLYOV. It was dozing… just sleeping in the sun. Quite happy… We hooted… the driver got out and hit it with a stick… It just chewed… I've never seen anything so contented.

My grandfather had a cow like that.

IVANOVSKY. Sergei, what is it?

KOROLYOV. My grandmother would tip the cream jug and I'd say, 'Just a little more, Nana, just a little more please.' Five of us, one cow. There never was a little more.

The Americans have a jug with no bottom, they tip it and tip it and the golden cream flows out... and never stops.

MISHIN. They refused us more funds.

KOROLYOV. No more funds. No more time.

I told them. I said, 'We can't rely on parachutes any more. We've risked the lives of brave boys time and again, floating them down on these... rags! Do you want to see a cosmonaut die!?'

MISHIN. If we have no more time...

IVANOVSKY. We can't develop another re-entry system and still meet our targets...

KOROLYOV (*cutting over him*). I'll do it! I will get it done!

My little eagles will land safe. Every one of them.

MISHIN *and* IVANOVSKY *look at each other, uncertain.* KOROLYOV *rounds on them.*

Why are you standing there! Get going! Get moving! Get working.

They hurry off. KOROLYOV *bangs the radio again, tuning it in. The signal returns, faint but distinct.*

SCHIRRA (*on radio*). Gemini 7, this is Gemini 6. We have an object, looks like a satellite going from north to south, probably in polar orbit. Looks like he might be going to re-enter soon. Stand by one. You just might pick up that thing.

KOROLYOV *is looking at the sky. Behind him the* ENGINEERS' *room forms. All the* ENGINEERS *working frantically.*

(*On radio.*) I see a command module and eight smaller modules in front. The pilot of the command module appears to be wearing a red suit.

On the radio, played erratically, 'Jingle Bells' on a xylophone and mouth organ.

The radio fades out on the astronauts' laughter.

KOROLYOV *rounds on the* ENGINEERS. *Frantic energy.*

KOROLYOV. Where are the reports I asked for!?

Everyone just keeps their heads down, working.

The stress reports! The stress reports on the new alloys! I asked for them yesterday. I made you responsible, you useless arse-wipe!

(*To* IVANOVSKY.) Come on! Come on! We're talking about a cosmonaut's safety! Where are my reports?

IVANOVSKY (*working*). They're not ready, Comrade Chief Designer.

KOROLYOV. Then you're fired.

Fix that. It's a piece of shit.

He throws the papers at him turns and sees MISHIN.

Stop gaping like a toad catching flies! What day is it?

MISHIN. It's eh…

KOROLYOV. Three months to launch! Yes? You remember? The date's lodged in there somewhere, is it!?

MISHIN. Of course, comrade…

KOROLYOV (*banging paperwork*). Then why isn't this done!? Who did you give it to?

A nervous ENGINEER *raises his hand.*

ENGINEER. I'm sorry, comrade, I didn't realise…

KOROLYOV. Oh, don't be sorry, shit, there's no time for that… Fix it!

He's shouting at the whole room again.

What's wrong with you all!? Staring at me like a field of sheep without the sense to chew grass! Work! Three months to launch! You think we can just wait on a flight of angels winging down to pull our Soyuz up to the Moon!? Work!

He points up at the rocket.

Comrade Komarov and the first cosmonaut are trusting their lives to us, to this. I don't care if your eyes are so dry you can't blink without screaming. I don't care if you're so tired you could fall asleep with your head in a bucket of nails! Work! Make them safe!

An ENGINEER *collapses.*

MISHIN *goes to her.*

What's wrong with her?

Is she alright?

MISHIN*'s helping the woman up.*

MISHIN. She's alright, SP.

KOROLYOV. Well, what's the matter with her?

IVANOVSKY. We've been working for thirty-two hours, SP.

KOROLYOV. Alright...

Alright...

Everyone get some rest. Get some food. Back here in six hours. A man can still work with only six hours' sleep in forty-eight. That's been proven in combat. Six! Understood? Not a minute more. Mishin, make sure they're here.

MISHIN. We'll all be here, Sergei.

As IVANOVSKY *passes,* KOROLYOV *snatches paperwork off him.*

KOROLYOV. Give that to me, I don't need to rest.

IVANOVSKY. But Sergei...

KOROLYOV. The drunken butchers are putting me flat on my back for twenty-four hours, you think I need to sleep now?

MISHIN, IVANOVSKY *and the* ENGINEERS *exit.*

KOROLYOV *looks at the paperwork.*

(*Muttering.*) That little pig's fart, what's he done here...?

(*Checking.*) No. No, he's right. Fuck him.

He rubs his eyes, slumping slightly. Exhausted.

YURI, LEONOV *and* KOMAROV *enter.*

YURI. Sergei?

KOROLYOV. What do you bastards want? You can't get in my clean spaceship with your filthy feet till I say she's ready.

KOMAROV. You asked us to come and see the work, Sergei Pavlovich?

KOROLYOV. I did?

Well, she's out there. Look all you like.

The COSMONAUTS *look up at the rocket.*

YURI. Same beauty.

KOROLYOV. Same piece of twisted shit. They sent the wrong sized clamps this time, oh, three hundred of them, two hundred and fifty more than we needed but none of the brainless oxen at the factory read the blueprints, and they're all full of cracks... Never mind, never mind... we'll get the parachute deployment right.

(*Showing them the angle with an imaginary capsule.*) A stable angle at re-entry! We'll fix it!

(*Re: the papers.*) Here, in my own hand, I'm doing it. That will be done. I promise you, Komarov.

YURI. Sergei...?

KOROLYOV (*stopping himself*). Oh, ignore me, boys.

Ignore me.

We've been here before. This is nothing. The lazy little slugs have all gone off and left me to drink on my own. Thank fuck you showed up.

KOROLYOV *produces a bottle and glasses. The* COSMONAUTS *gape in astonishment.*

YURI. You're drinking.

KOROLYOV. Yes, tonight I feel like having a drink. Is that alright with you, First Cosmonaut?

YURI. I could force one down.

KOROLYOV *pours them all drinks*.

KOROLYOV. Alright… to the new leader of the glorious
republic of Soviets… Comrade Brezhnev…

They all raise their glasses, 'Comrade Brezhnev'.

YURI (*pointing meaningfuly at the ceiling*). And I'm sure he'll
be glad to hear us wish him good health.

LEONOV *and* KOMAROV *look at* YURI. *They look at the
ceiling.*

They look at KOROLYOV *for confirmation.*

KOMAROV (*whisper*). You think they've put bugs…?

KOROLYOV. You think they've only just done that? There'll
be fifteen years of tapes in a cellar somewhere.

He shrugs.

When I was sentenced I never had said anything against the
party. What difference does it make now?

YURI. You never talk about that.

KOROLYOV. Being in the Gulag?

YURI. Yes.

KOROLYOV. Ah, but I never drink.

*He grins at them. He takes a big swig and tops them all up.
The* DOCTOR *enters and speaks from the shadows.*

DOCTOR. Comrade Korolyov, you've got surgery in the
morning.

KOROLYOV (*impatient*). Yes, yes, yes…

DOCTOR. You shouldn't drink.

KOROLYOV. So I'll save the party the price of anaesthetic!
Leave us alone, witch.

The DOCTOR *exits.*

YURI. They're not putting you in that VIP hospital at the
Kremlin, are they?

KOROLYOV. Of course they are.

YURI (*getting up*). Right, I told them I wasn't having that. They're useless up there!

KOROLYOV (*to the others*). The first cosmonaut told them...

YURI. They never get any practice! Bunch of ancient dodderers falling over with the weight of their medals, they haven't a clue...

KOROLYOV. They are operating on my arse.

LEONOV. What?

KOROLYOV. I have polyps on my lower intestine. The honoured doctors, at the Kremlin hospital for heroes and dignitaries, will be performing surgery up my arse.

LEONOV. Best place for them.

KOROLYOV. That's what I think.

KOMAROV *looks nervously at the ceiling.*

KOMAROV. Comrade Chief Designer...

KOROLYOV. Oh relax, Komarov! They know what I think.

YURI (*to* LEONOV). He's pissed already, can you believe it?

LEONOV. Well, he's had no practice, has he?

KOROLYOV. Did I ever tell you boys about the day I started walking to Moscow?

YURI. No.

KOROLYOV. A letter came. They would review my case... if I could get to Moscow... I started walking. The sun was coming up. I remember the sun in my eyes. I pushed snow onto my wounds... they stopped bleeding.

At the end of the day a truck came past. I asked the driver to take me to the port. He wanted my coat. I had to give him my coat.

But when we reached the port the last ship south had sailed...

It was forty-five below and I had nowhere to sleep. No one would let me in. I reported to the army barracks, but they wouldn't arrest me...

I thought I must just keep moving or I'll die… so I just started walking… round and round… I just kept walking.

It was the strangest thing, boys, the strangest thing. I was walking along this path through the snow, I'd no coat, I hadn't eaten for two days… And suddenly there it was – a loaf. Lying on the snow in front of me. A loaf. A warm loaf.

I ate it so fast I got hiccups. Then I crept back into the army prison and slept under the bed where they couldn't see me. I hid there all winter, crawling out after dark to steal food, till the ice melted and the ships were moving south again. All my life I've wondered where that bread came from. It was just enough to keep me walking, that's all I needed. You see?

He grips KOMAROV*'s hand.*

I don't ever stop. I'd be dead already if I'd ever lain down but I never do. I can do it all, Komarov, I won't close my eyes for the next ten years, till all my little eagles are out there, and I'll keep you safe whatever else happens to you.

YURI. You're pissed, Sergei.

KOROLYOV (*surprised*). I am.

YURI. I think we better leave you.

He kisses KOROLYOV*'s head and rumples his hair gently.*

KOROLYOV. Hey! I'm still drinking!

LEONOV. Goodnight, Sergei Pavlovich.

KOROLYOV. Yes, yes. Goodnight then. Leave me the sugar.

LEONOV. The sugar?

YURI. There isn't any sugar, Sergei Pavlovich.

KOROLYOV. Then find me some!

The COSMONAUTS *look at each other and laugh.*
LEONOV *takes a little twist of sugar out of his pocket. He gives it to* KOROLYOV.

LEONOV. There you are, Comrade Chief Designer. A present.

KOROLYOV. Thanks. Alright. Off you go.

YURI, KOMAROV *and* LEONOV *exit. The* OLD MAN *walks out of the shadows towards* KOROLYOV.

OLD MAN. Dip it in vodka, melt it on your tongue, then drain the rest and think of me.

KOROLYOV *dunks the sugar lump in his glass then washes it down with vodka.*

KOROLYOV. Men like us can travel beyond the Moon.

OLD MAN. If you say so, son. Just don't forget me, eh?

KOROLYOV. I've never forgotten you.

OLD MAN. Good. That's good.

The DOCTOR *enters.*

KOROLYOV. Here she is. Here we all are, together again.

DOCTOR. What are you talking about, you old fool?

The OLD MAN *slowly exits.*

KOROLYOV. Is it time?

DOCTOR. The car will be here soon.

KOROLYOV *reaches out to her. She takes his hand.*

KOROLYOV. Will you stay with me, witch?

DOCTOR. As long as they let me.

KOROLYOV. I've been thinking... we should train a poet to be a cosmonaut. Someone who can really tell us all what's up there. Write that down. I'll get them working on that tomorrow.

DOCTOR. I'm not your secretary.

KOROLYOV. Didn't I get you your apartment?

DOCTOR. No. You did not.

KOROLYOV. Shit, have they not sorted that out yet? I'll get right on that.

DOCTOR. Uh-huh.

KOROLYOV. They're going to make me sleep, aren't they?

DOCTOR. It'll be alright. It'll be warm, it'll be quiet and I won't let you stay asleep too long. I promise.

Scene Eight

The launch pad.

YURI *and* KOMAROV *are standing looking up at the rocket.* KOMAROV *hands* YURI *a letter.*

KOMAROV. This is for my wife.

KOMAROV *starts walking to the ladder to climb up into the rocket. He's escorted by two* TECHNICIANS.

YURI *hesitates then runs forward and tries to stop them.*

YURI. Vladimir, stop!

The TECHNICIANS *hold* YURI *back.*

Get off me! Comrade Lieutenant Komarov is not well… Look at him! Look at him, man! He's sick!

TECHNICIAN. Comrade Komarov has been medically approved to fly.

YURI. I'm the first cosmonaut. I'm the first cosmonaut and I'm ordering you to take the lieutenant for more tests.

TECHNICIAN. I can't do that, comrade. I've got my orders.

YURI. I'm giving you new orders!

TECHNICIAN. I can't do that, Comrade Gagarin.

YURI. Get off me! I'm taking over this mission. I consider Cosmonaut Komarov unfit to fly and I'm taking over this mission.

TECHNICIAN. The back-up cosmonaut has been ordered to stand down.

YURI. I am the first cosmonaut and I'm telling you…!

TECHNICIAN (*cutting him off*). You've been ordered to stand down!

The roar of the rocket launch and blinding light.

Scene Nine

Command bunker at the launch pad.

MISHIN *is on the microphone.* YURI *and* LEONOV *are looking up.* KOMAROV *hangs above them.*

LEONOV (*to* MISHIN). He's going to start falling out of orbit.

MISHIN (*on microphone*). Comrade Lieutenant... it is my official duty to report...

KOMAROV. Yes...

MISHIN (*on microphone*)....as we have been repeatedly unable to engage the solar panel...

KOMAROV. Yes...

MISHIN (*on microphone*)....that your mission must be terminated now...

KOMAROV. Yes, yes, I know all this, yes...

MISHIN (*on microphone*). Are you ready to attempt re-entry now, Comrade Lieutenant?

KOMAROV *laughs in terror.*

KOMAROV. This fucking ship... this fucking ship, nothing works, nothing I touch works...

MISHIN (*on microphone*). Do you need some more time, comrade?

KOMAROV. Yes! Yes! I want more time! I want my life! I want my whole life!

Oh shit...

MISHIN (*on microphone*). Would you like to speak to your wife again?

KOMAROV (*nearly losing it*). No… no… don't… leave her alone now.

MISHIN (*on microphone*). You're a hero. You're a hero of the Soviet Republic and – (*Nearly losing it himself.*) you're a hero.

KOMAROV. Yes, yes, yes… Alright… Can we… Can I do it… Can I still? Is there any chance?

LEONOV. If he can keep the spinning under control…

KOMAROV. She just spins round like a duck with one wing! Oh shit…

(*To himself.*) Come on! I can hold her I can… stabilise.

MISHIN (*on microphone*). We're ready for you to attempt re-entry.

KOMAROV. Tell Yuri… tell him better me than him… it's alright, Yuri…

This hits YURI *like a blow.* LEONOV *holds onto him.*

MISHIN (*on microphone*). We're ready now.

KOMAROV. Alright… alright… I'll hold her… I'll hold her…

I've got her… I've got her… shit… I can't get control…!

MISHIN (*on microphone*). Thirty seconds till parachute deployment.

KOMAROV. Alright… alright… I can… yes… holding her… yes… got her… got her… that's right… just there… just there…

MISHIN (*on microphone*). Twenty seconds…

KOMAROV. We can do it… come on, Soyuz… we can do this…

MISHIN (*on microphone*). Ten seconds…

KOMAROV. Just… hold this angle… just hold on…

MISHIN (*on microphone*). Well done, cosmonaut! You're coming home. Parachute deployed…

It fails.

Cosmonaut confirm parachute deployment. Confirm
parachute deployment. Confirm parachute deployment.

KOMAROV. It failed. The parachute failed! I'm spinning! It
can't open! The parachute can't open!

It failed!

Oh, Korolyov save me. Korolyov, please! Come back from
the grave and get me out of this!

(*Starting to lose it.*) You promised me! Korolyov, you
promised me you'd get my parachute open! You promised
me!!!!

I'm dead! I'm dead!

KOMAROV *plummets towards the ground.*

Oh, you fuckers you've killed me! You've killed me! Fuck
you all!

A blinding flash. An explosion.

Scene Ten

An interrogation room somewhere in the USA.

A big Stars and Stripes.

The DOCTOR *sits smoking, listening to the tape of*
KOMAROV's *last moments. It's really upsetting her, but she
keeps it all in.*

An American airforce officer, STEVE, *sits opposite her.*

*We hear the same dialogue from the end of the previous scene,
but this time in Russian.*

MISHIN. *Tavarish kosmonavt! Pad-tvyerditye, shto vishel
parashiut…*

KOMAROV. *Atkazal. Atkazal parashiut. Nye raskrivayetsya!
Parashiut nye raskrivayetsya!*

Atkazal!

O, Karalyov, spasi minya! Karalyov! Prashu tibya…
Vyerniss, vaskryesni, spasi minya! Ti zhe mnye abyeshal!
Karalyov, ti zhe mnye abyeshal, shto raskroyetsya!
Abyeshal!!!!

Pagib! Pagib ya! Ookh, svolochi, ubili minya! Ubili! Mat(sh)
vashu…

The tape stops.

STEVE. My colleagues here want to know who the cosmonaut is talking about on the tape.

DOCTOR. I want an apartment. They promised me.

STEVE. Well. If they promised you…

DOCTOR. What?

STEVE. As long as the quality of the information is good enough.

DOCTOR. I can't go back now. I need an apartment here. I need US citizenship.

STEVE. Like I said. If they like what they hear…

DOCTOR. What do they want to know?

STEVE. Who's Korolyov?

DOCTOR. You don't know?

STEVE. No.

DOCTOR. He was the chief designer.

STEVE. Of the Soyuz programme?

DOCTOR. Soyuz, Vostok, Sputnik… You didn't know?

STEVE. He did it all?

DOCTOR. Yes.

STEVE. Just one man?

DOCTOR. Yes, just one man. You had Von Brahn and all the other German scientists and all your thousands of workers and billions of dollars and we had Sergei Pavlovich and convicts and some university students. So what? We got there, didn't we? Quicker than you.

STEVE. National pride, that's great, don't want to go home though, do you? What's he doing now?

The DOCTOR *says nothing.*

What's this Korolyov planning now?

DOCTOR. He's dead.

They wouldn't let me talk to the surgeons...

The DOCTOR *is close to breaking down. She holds it in.*

He only wanted five years. He thought he could do it all.

They only found Komarov's heel bone. That's all that was left.

I want an apartment. With sun. I want sunlight.

STEVE. When did Korolyov die?

DOCTOR. They wouldn't listen. It wasn't just his heart... In the Gulag, I saw the guard hit Sergei... it drove his jaw up into the base of his skull... and it was never treated, it set badly... so his airway was restricted, there was so much scar tissue... They didn't know, they wouldn't let me stay with him... they put the tube in badly, he wasn't getting enough air... and his heart... his heart was always weak... I told him so...

(*Losing it a bit.*) Oh, but he didn't have a heart condition. Officially, on paper his heart was strong, that's what had been agreed!

She gets herself together.

STEVE. So he's dead.

DOCTOR. Yes.

STEVE. And you worked closely with him?

DOCTOR. For years.

We all loved him.

STEVE. Well, I think that's what they're going to want to ask you about.

DOCTOR. Why?

STEVE. Look, they just brought me in because I speak Russian and I know the space programme. Someone else will be asking you questions now.

But I tell you something, I'm going to be first in line to hear the answers.

One man?

DOCTOR. Yes.

STEVE. Sputnik got me dreaming of getting up there. He changed it all. He changed everything I thought and felt when I looked up at the sky. Changed it for ever.

STEVE *moves to exit.*

DOCTOR. But... my apartment. They promised me an apartment.

STEVE. Everyone gets an apartment.

The DOCTOR *stands looking out at the sky.* KOROLYOV *comes to stand behind her.*

DOCTOR. Are you there? Can you hear me?

KOROLYOV. No.

DOCTOR. I can feel you.

KOROLYOV. I won't lie down.

DOCTOR. The dead should lie down. That's the least they should do.

KOROLYOV. Are you still sorry, that you saved me?

DOCTOR. No. I'm not.

They say you changed the whole sky and everything under it, Sergei Pavlovich.

What does that mean?

End of play.